# 2nd Edition

# HOW ATTRACTING WOMEN REALLY WORKS

## by Marc Summers

# CONTENTS

# ABOUT MARC SUMMERS

Hey it's Marc Summers. Before you start reading this book, I want to take a minute to let you know that my job is to help you and you're only learning what works. I never claim to know everything but I've had a lot of success with women, dating, and relationships and I'm sharing what I've learned through personal experience, research, experimenting, and becoming friends with smart and capable men who attract women easily.

No one likes screwing up and embarrassing themselves with women and I'm here to help you avoid that as much as possible. I do that by working tirelessly to ensure you're getting the very best tips, help, and solutions that I have to offer. The more I can help you move in the right direction, the more you'll become the man women actually want. My rule is if I haven't seen it work, I won't waste your time teaching it to you. If you have questions, email me directly at **marc@majorleaguedating.com** and I'll gladly help you out.

# DISCLAIMER

I have to be upfront with you before you begin this book to make sure we're clear. I am not a doctor, psychologist, psychiatrist, therapist, healer, etc. I dropped out of college way before becoming a licensed doctor and psychologist when I realized that, one, a scary number of psychologists commit suicide and, two, when my professor tried teaching us how to exercise our body using our mind and without having to move. It was a complete freakshow I wanted no part of.

Legally, and so we have an understanding, I have to tell you that this book is intended for entertainment purposes ONLY. It's not to be used as substitution for help from a licensed professional. If you need actual help or medication, this book won't solve that problem. I'm also not claiming that what you will learn will absolutely work for you. Everyone is different and everyone gets different results.

I firmly believe you get out what you put into it. If you seek to fully understand what I say in this book and compare it to your own personal intelligence, judgement, common sense, and what you figure to be true about life and the world, you will get a lot out of it. If you start this book and automatically dismiss me as a jackass idiot because you read something that makes you uncomfortable, then you probably won't get a lot out of it. It's all up to you. I can't force you to master this information.

Let me be clear - the information contained in this book is what has worked FOR ME to help me attract women. It's what I've witnessed with my own two eyes and from information I've processed for years in my own brain. What I've put into this book for your gain is the result of my own personal thought and judgement. If you don't agree with me on everything, that's perfectly fine. I don't expect you to. But it's important to make sure we're on the same page before you begin this book.

# CREDIT WHERE IT'S DUE

The minute she heard her ex was getting out of jail, my girlfriend of a year began packing her things and told me she was leaving. As she repeatedly walked past me from the bedroom to the front door, tossing her bags onto the floor, she ignored me like I no longer existed or mattered. Every time she passed, she uncomfortably exhaled and looked the other way as if anticipating me saying or doing something annoying. Instead of keeping it together, being strong, and analyzing the severity of the situation, I attempted to guilt trip her into changing her mind by getting myself worked up, making tears come down my face, sniffling loudly, and looking her in the eyes as she walked by. Upon seeing my face and recognizing exactly what I was doing, she shook her head and laughed to herself in disbelief. It was pretty pathetic.

She had every right to feel however she felt. Looking back on it, if I were in her shoes, I would've felt the same way and left too. This was happening because over the last year of our relationship, the mask of who I pretended to be had faded away and revealed a clueless, weak, emotional, and approval-seeking guy who didn't understand attraction.

When she left, I continued the clueless nice guy act and carried her bags down to the taxi for her while she stood there and watched me continue to make a fool of myself. I still cringe when I think about it because it wasn't like, "Here, bitch. I'll do the work for you so you can get out of my life faster." It was more like, "No matter what you do, I'm still terrified of your disapproval and I don't want you thinking I'm not a nice guy."

Even while getting the poorest results possible, I still couldn't turn off the logical, ineffective, and manipulative nice guy act. She had 99% of the power and instead of ending the relationship with my last bit of dignity, I still bent over backwards to give her the 1% of power I had left.

THE BEST DATING TIPS, HELP, & SOLUTIONS – MAJORLEAGUEDATING.COM

The purpose of sharing my embarrassing story with you and revealing exactly how pathetic I was with women and how little I understood attraction is to help you understand you're not the only guy who doesn't have it all figured out. In fact, I would say 95% of men, and that's being generous, aren't able to clearly explain what you're about to learn in this book. My story happened many years ago, but it has never happened again because, from that day forward, I spent well over a decade observing and studying women's behavior and learning from other experienced men about how attracting women actually works.

One of those men is Eben Pagan, also known by his pseudonym, David Deangelo. If it wasn't for him, I wouldn't be able to teach you any of this. After she left and I was down in the dumps, feeling sorry for myself, acting like a victim, and even, contemplating suicide, I downloaded his online book *Attraction Isn't A Choice* and began my decade long effort into understand attraction better.

David developed the idea that putting her on a pedestal, being the nicest guy she's ever met, kissing her ass, and buying flowers is a major and ignorant gamble because it doesn't create deep and real attraction and you're giving her power over yourself and the relationship. That, if you're doing what 99% of men don't do, which is aligning your thoughts, words, behavior, and habits with what she primitively and biologicaly responds to, her attraction for you multiplies, she begins to feel things she's never felt before, and she can't control it or turn it off. This major change in your thinking and behavior creates such a powerful shift in your interactions with women that it betters your ability to control the outcome of the friendship and relationship.

Once I understood this basic idea, I was able to identify everything I was doing wrong with women and the experience from it has helped me to further clarify and expand upon it for your knowledge, wisdom, and gain.

# WHY YOU SHOULD KNOW THIS

This idea of "attraction isn't a choice" is the single most important thing you need to know to turn your dating life around, attract the women you actually want, and, ultimately, become happier about your relationship with them. It ties EVERYTHING together. It's the key to the better dating life all men want and the piece of the puzzle most men never find. Without it, you're destined to a mediocre dating and love life and your mind will remain filled with more questions and confusion than answers.

The techniques and crutches of pickup artists might help you catch her attention, say the right words, move her around the room at the right times and to the right spots, and charm her pants off by pretending to be someone you're not, but if you don't understand how attraction really works and why it's important to know, then success will be fleeting. In a short time, she'll see you as an imposter and her gut instinct will force her to separate herself from you and your sketchy relationship with her.

Becoming the nicest, most empathetic, and most considerate guy, telling her every day how beautiful you think she is, and showing her your sensitive and caring side won't work without this missing knowledge. Instead of thinking you're a great guy, she'll see you as fake, weak, wimpy, and desperate. A man living a lie to get approval, sex, and love.

Being a tyrannical jerk, overdoing your delusional and concocted "alpha male" positioning, and acting above women may give the appearance of strength and competence and may even get you laid more often, but it won't keep women in your life. Their attraction will turn into confusion, disapproval, and fear as you display apparent major psychological issues.

No shortcut, technique, or trick replaces this information and nothing contributes more to massive and permanent dating life improvements.

# WHY IS ATTRACTION SO FRUSTRATING AND CONFUSING?

When I was about 14 or 15 years old and started taking girls and relationships more seriously, I did the same things I think most guys do today when they're inexperienced with women and don't understand attraction or how it works. I was terrified of rejection, didn't know what to think, how to behave, or what to say, and winged it as much as possible. I complemented regularly, told exaggerated stories and showed off to impress, kissed ass and sought approval, spent money to show how much I liked them, and shared my emotions and feelings in hopes of taking things to the "next level". And you know what, a lot of it worked! I could pretend to be cooler, nicer, and different than I actually was and because these girls were still young, naïve, and didn't have a lot of experience with men, they totally bought it. Years later, I failed so miserably with my girlfriend who left me for her ex-boyfriend getting out of jail because I didn't understand or take into consideration that older women aren't stupid and don't fall for the same games they did when they were younger. She'd seen the tricks, manipulation, techniques, and shortcuts before and she only felt convinced that I didn't "get it" or know how attraction really worked. It's not something she could explain with words but she felt it deep down and knew that what she was feeling wasn't what she wanted to feel. She could express her frustration and disappointment, but she couldn't explain it to me in such a way that I could correct it and prevent it from coming up again.

The reason attracting women becomes so frustrating and confusing for us as we get older is because many of us still believe the same tricks, manipulation, techniques, and shortcuts that worked on girls in high school should still work with women today. When we discover the hard way that these things actually don't work anymore, we develop a lot of anger, frustration, and resentment toward women, dating, and relationships. We're mad that things have changed and it's not as easy as we want it to be.

The first step to overcoming this frustration and confusion is, as I've said before, understanding that adult women don't respond the same way to the tricks, techniques, and shortcuts as they did when they were younger. Most women go through a brutal and painful process of overcoming their naivete. They experience falling madly in love for the first time, eating up all of the promises, flattery, and attention, thinking he's the only guy for them and it's going to last forever, and then it all comes crashing down when they experience their first devastating heartbreak. The deep hurt, a hurt they've never felt, forever alters their perspective on men and relationships and awakens their skepticism. For most women, it's not a PTSD kind of hurt that makes them forever hate men and relationships, but a mildly jolting emotional trauma that wakes them up to the reality that they're not Cinderella, life isn't a fairy tale, and they have to protect themselves from being exploited by men. The experience teaches many women that men can be manipulative, deceiptful, and, some, will go to great lengths to get what they want and don't care who gets hurt in the process. That wall and "bitch shield" you sense and feel when talking to women who seem uninterested, most of the time, didn't exist before that first major heartbreak. As she matures, snaps out of that naïve mindset, and the emotional magic carpet ride comes to an end, she discovers she has a special "rejection power" that she must use to protect herself from getting hurt like that again.

The next time you find yourself getting frustrated and confused because you're not making progress and she's not responding the way you want, keep in mind that, first, she's not a naïve teenager anymore and the childish manipulation and games are less likely to work and, second, you have to work around the wall she uses to protect herself. It's not there because she gets an ego boost from watching you struggle to get around it; it's there because she's been lied to, screwed over, and hurt, she doesn't like how it feels, and she's not going to just drop it because it makes you uncomfortable, frustrated, and confused. She's not going to drop it just because you make promises and try to convince her of what a wonderful guy you are. Instead of getting angry about it, invest time and energy working on and learning how to get her to lower her wall for you.

Another thing that makes women and dating frustrating and confusing and pisses off a lot of men, and I'm sure you can relate to this, is women seem to be full of crap. They say they want one thing but then go after another. They say one thing and then DO another. They tell you they feel a certain way one minute and the next they've changed their mind! And when questioned about it, they can't seem to offer any logical or reasonable explanations! It's like you're damned if you do and damned if you don't.

Attraction isn't as straightforward as you want it to be when you don't understand it but it becomes clearer and easier to pull off once you do. Attraction is a strategy, just like poker, on how to play the hand that you have the best you can. You have to know when to fold, when to throw more chips in the pot, and when to go all in. You have to read her emotions, look for her tells, and figure out what she's really thinking. In poker, you pay attention to human behavior and make your moves based on what you're observing and the better you get at it, the more successful you are. You have to look at what you have, what you think is going on with the other player, and make strategic decisions moving forward. If you go all in every single hand, you'll always be broke. If you stay too consistent, you'll never win as much as you want to.

THE BEST DATING TIPS, HELP, & SOLUTIONS – MAJORLEAGUEDATING.COM

# PART 1: 10

# ATTRACTION

# DESTROYING

# MINDSETS

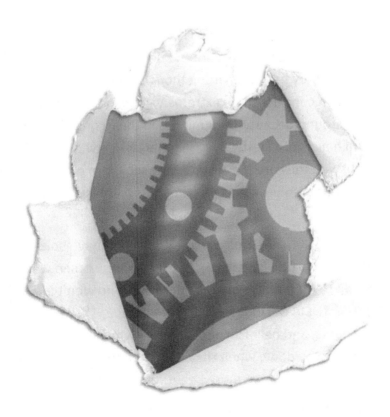

It's important to learn and know which mindsets kill attraction because if you're not mentally in the right place when interacting with women, then you really can't achieve the success you actually want with them. It doesn't matter how good the techniques and shortcuts are that you learned from watching pickup artist videos and reading their books. If your mind isn't put together, meaning you have trained your mind with effective thoughts and beliefs, no shortcut will save you. Once you're out of tricks, your true mindset and personality will shine through and she'll likely see you as an imposter or a fraud. She'll see who you really are as a person and whatever attraction she felt will vanish. Before you can take action and make amazing things happen with women, your mind has to be pointed in the right direction.

Again, your mindset is EVERYTHING. There are men worth tens of millions of dollars who can't keep women around because their mind is in the wrong place and they have the wrong thoughts and beliefs. There are men who women consider to be extremely good looking but they can't keep women around because their mind is in the wrong place and their thoughts and beliefs are ineffective. There are men who are FAMOUS and women know who they are the minute they see them but they STILL can't keep women attracted because their thoughts and beliefs are weak and ineffective.

At the same time, there are men who are dirt poor, have holes in their shoes, and live in horrible conditions YET they have women who call like crazy, show up to their house on a regular basis, and won't leave them alone BECAUSE THEIR MIND IS IN THE RIGHT PLACE. They have the right attitude, thoughts, and beliefs. There are men who hit ALL of the branches on the way down when they fell out of the ugly tree and yet they attract and date women more beautiful than you can imagine.

Your mindset is the most important tool you have to attract women.

# #1: THINKING YOU HAVE TO BE NICE NO MATTER WHAT

It's one thing to be nice and another to be overly nice. Nice is just a gesture of courtesy and politeness. There's nothing wrong with being nice and it does a lot of good when it comes from the right place and the right mindset. But, when nice comes from the mindset of trying to manipulate women into giving you something in return, it's cowardly, naive, and ineffective. You're using your niceness to decieve and paint a picture of something that isn't true. You're not being authentic and, instead, putting on an act and being someone you're not to get something in return - whether it be attention, approval, admiration, sex, love, etc.

But, here's the thing most men don't know or understand - YOU DO NOT HAVE TO BE OVERLY NICE TO WOMEN to get what you want from them. A little bit nice is good enough and even if you're in between being a jerk and a sweet guy or just being totally neutral and not caring about anything too much, THAT'S GOOD ENOUGH. Neutral is 10x better than overly nice because at least neutral doesn't make women run away. Instead, neutral makes women more interested. Overly nice makes you look weird and sketchy. Most women who get lots of male attention, if their honest enough, will tell you they are sick and tired of men being overly nice and they just want men to be real and authentic.

Overly nice is a weak mindset because it comes from a place of fear, insecurity, desperation, and neediness. Overly nice doesn't earn you extra points and when you go out of your way to be extra nice, you're only setting yourself back and making your job in attracting her and dating her that much harder.

Think about it - people aren't normally THAT nice. If everyone in your life was overly nice to you all of the time, you'd be punching people in the face! It would drive you crazy because it's so FAKE and weird. When anyone is being overly nice, there's always a reason behind it - they want to sell you something or they want something from you. When they don't want anything from you, they're just neutral and "whatever" about it, aren't they? But when they want your money or a favor, the FAKE personality comes out to manipulate you into doing what they want you to do.

The alarm that goes off in your mind when someone is being fake and overly nice is the same alarm that goes off in her mind when you're doing it to her. She knows something is up because there's NO WAY you're actually that nice and perfect. It's just way too sketchy to be real.

When you value yourself, have a sense of self-worth, handle your own emotional needs, and don't care about getting validation from anyone, the overly nice act goes away on it's own. One day you're talking to a woman and you have the realization that you're not saying and doing the dumb shit you've always said and done to get women to like you. You're just being yourself and you really don't care as much what she thinks about it. It's a moment of intense awareness and freedom. It feels good.

A big reason women are attracted to jerks is because jerks don't care as much about women's approval. They know they're a jerk, they're comfortable being a jerk, and they know women respond to the jerk attitude better than the nice guy act. The moment I realized I was way too nice and it was making me look extremely weak and vulnerable, I decided to intentionally go ALL THEY WAY to the other side of the spectrum and see if being a jerk actually got me better results. What happened was amazing! Even though being a jerk did turn a lot of women off and cause them to call me cocky and arrogant, I no longer gave off the impression of a weak and scared little bitch. Women saw me as being mentally and physically tougher, stronger, pickier, and more unique. The same amount of women that were turned off by it were also extremely turned on by it. My dating life took off like a rocket because my attitude when from "I want something from you" to "I want you and I don't care what you think about me". Is being a jerk the best approach? Probably not BUT it works WAY better than being overly nice.

What works best is being somewhere in the middle. You want to be a nice and approachable person but, at the same time, you don't want to give the impression that you're desperate and weak and women can take advantage of you. You want to have the mindset of, "I'm cool and I'll be friendly as long as you're cool and friendly too. The minute you think about playing games with me or treating me like I'm stupid is when I quit being friendly and I start being a jerk."

What I do is simple, it works very well, and I have this same attitude and mindset with my girlfriend, family, friends, and co-workers, and even my daughter. It's across the board. NO ONE is exempt. Even though I'm relaxed, friendly, joking around, and having a good time, I'm not afraid to be a little skeptical and ask questions when necessary. This communicates I'm valuable and not mentally weak and gullible. I don't buy everything women say just because they're pretty and have a hot body. I don't buy everything anyone says just because they have something to offer me. I'm on my toes and paying attention.

When you're overly nice because you want something from her, you're too afraid to call her out on her bullshit or something that sounds like bullshit because you don't want to ruin the opportunity. You're too afraid to question her and challenge her and, instead, just give her approval and go along with whatever she says hoping that you'll get "lucky". Wrong approach. Being skeptical, asking questions, and challenging women builds 10X more attraction than being overly nice because you're giving her something to do and you're keeping her from getting bored. She doesn't feel like you're being her little servant boy who kisses her feet and ass every chance you get.

After all of these years of crashing and burning, if you're still using "nice" as your main strategy, it's because most women aren't going to tell you how your overly nice and fake personality actually makes them feel. It's an awkward conversation they refuse to have. It puts them in a weird position and being so brutally honest gives them tons of anxiety. Keep in mind that we live in a society where most people are fake with themselves and fake with eachother. If most people won't be totally honest with themselves, they won't be totally honest with you. They'd rather just avoid all of the potential drama and weirdness at all costs. Instead, they just put on a fake smile, show fake enthusiasm, and act polite despite how disgusted they really feel inside. The stories and excuses as to why you can't have their number and why they can't go out with you are, 90% of the time, completely made up because they don't want to say, "No. You're weird and too nice and I'm not interested."

You have no more excuses to be overly nice. It doesn't matter if your mom told you to always be overly nice, it isn't effective and only backfires on you. I challenge you, not to be a jerk, but to quit being so nice. Have conversations with women and keep a straight face. Wipe the dumb grin off of your face when you're around pretty women. Stop vomiting up all of the lame compliments that aren't going to do anything for you. Stop treating women like they're godesses. Stop apologizing and thinking it's earning you brownie points. Let them catch you glancing at their butt and boobs. Let them catch you checking them out. Instead of looking at women like they're above you and you're below them, look at them like you're on their level and they have something to prove to YOU.

# #2: THINKING YOU NEED TO IMPRESS HER

Women being impressed and feeling the type of attraction that makes them want to have sex with you, date you, be your girlfriend, marry you, and have kids with you are two completely different things.

The men that women are the most impressed with are the men who are impressed with themselves and aren't actively seeking to impress other people. I'll say it again, the men that impress women the most are the ones who aren't concerned with impressing other people. Drill that into your mind. It's had a tremedous effect on my dating life and the results I get with women. When I sought to impress, it's because I wasn't impressed with myself and so I wanted OTHER PEOPLE to be impressed with me so I would be impressed with how impressed they were of me. That's not a tongue twister. Because I wasn't feeling excited and proud of myself, I sought to fill that void inside of me by impressing women and others. I used their approval to TEMPORARILY make myself feel better about myself. Once that short lived dose of approval that I got from impressing people wore off, I was back to trying to impress women. It was a vicious cycle that ate away at my happiness and self-esteem.

The truth is, my dating life suffered tremendously and the only women who felt real attraction for me were losers. Harsh, but true. Women who had nothing going for themselves and who's lives were out-of-control. Women who only took value instead of adding it. They were impressed because their standards were so damn low that pretty much ANYTHING and ANYONE impressed them but I was too dumb to see that at the time.

My dating life changed when I sought out to impress myself. I asked myself, "OK, Marc, what are you unimpressed with yourself about?" My answer to myself was, "I don't think my body is as muscular and defined as it could be. I could be physically stronger. I don't think I'm as smart as I could be. I don't think I'm making the best decisions. I don't like how I handle my money. I don't like how I conduct myself at work. I don't like how I communicate with people. I don't like that I brag about what I did YEARS ago. I don't like what time I go to bed and wake up. I don't like how much I'm not accomplishing. I don't like the quality of women I'm dating. I know I can do better." The list went on and on. I felt if I could impress myself, then things in my life would get easier. I would feel more pride in who I am and what I'm about.

One by one I began to focus on my internal goals rather than external and as I got each one handled and under control, the less of a need I felt to impress women and others. The less of a need I felt to run my mouth and tell people how great I am, what I do for a living, how much money I make, or what I've accomplished. Being proud of MYSELF gave me the dose of approval I was looking for in others. Get it? You're looking for that dose of approval when you're trying to impress others but what you really need is the approval from YOURSELF! The approval you want is EXACTLY the same whether it's coming from women, other people, or yourself. The difference is that one is way more effective than the other.

Approval from other people who don't care about you as much as you think gets you more and more addicted to getting more of it. Approval and being impressed with yourself makes you feel better and better and gets you more and more addicted to doing better and improving yourself. One is very negative and destructive, the other is purely beneficial.

The guy who is losing with women asks himself, "What's the next thing I can do to impress her so I can hopefully get laid?" They guy who's impressing himself and attracting all the women asks, "OK, where am I not impressing myself? Where can I improve and become better?"

THE BEST DATING TIPS, HELP, & SOLUTIONS – MAJORLEAGUEDATING.COM

Impressing other people makes you look like a moron that women avoid and impressing yourself helps you become the person your friends and family look up to. It makes women feel attraction and want to be part of your life. There's no shortcutting or tricking the system.

Draw a line, pick a side, and get on it. You're either going to continue wasting time and energy going out of your way to impress other people who don't give a shit about you because you're too lazy to impress yourself or you're going to make an investment in impressing yourself and quit caring about how much other people admire you.

This includes social media, taking selfies, and all of the ignorant behaviors that are running rampant today. If you're on a boat with your family, then put the phone down and just spend time with your family. Cherish that moment. Stop taking selfies and posting them on social media to impress and make everyone feel your life is better than theirs. Chances are, it's not even your boat! It's your dad's and as Gary Vaynerchuk says, you're "punking other people on your dad's shit"!

If you're investing your precious time into these type of behaviors and you're struggling to attract women, that's why. You're trying to create an illusion of how great your life is and how much of a wannabe celebrity you are. Real celebrities have OTHER PEOPLE taking pictures of them, they're running away from the cameras, and they want privacy. Wannabe celebrities who seek to impress women and others take pictures of themselves, they're holding the camera, and they want NO privacy.

If you want to attract women and make them feel things they usually don't feel for other men, then do as much as you can to impress yourself and stop seeking attention for it. When you have a lot of good things happening in your life and you're not talking or bragging about it, IT'S OBVIOUS! When you talk about it, people don't believe you anyways. When you don't, people use their imagination and admire you.

# #3: CARING TOO MUCH IF SHE LIKES YOU OR NOT

This may not make total sense the first time you hear it but if you want women to actually like you and feel attraction for you, you have to stop caring what they think about you and how much they like you. Yes, it IS important how much women like you but it's as equally important not to preoccupy your mind with how she feels. It's important to clear up your mind as much as possible and keep it that way. Do you want her to like you? Of course your do! It's a natural human desire. But, the more time and energy you invest into consciously thinking about it, the more likely you are to become nervous and anxious and screw the whole thing up!

The most effective mindset is, "I like this girl. I think she's cool. I like hanging out with her and spending time with her but if she doesn't like me as much as I like her, I refuse to let it ruin my day." It's important to accept that not everyone is going to like you as much as you like them. It's a part of life you will NEVER change. If you like yourself, enjoy spending time with yourself, and think you're a good person who women like being around and spending time with, then how much they like you shouldn't be an issue. It shouldn't consume your mind and make you unhappy. The more you like yourself and the better you treat yourself, the more likely women are to like you the same way and treat you the same way. The shortcut to attraction that most guys aren't getting is people always treat you the way they see you treat yourself. If you want women to accept you and like you for who you are, you have to first accept yourself and like yourself for who you are. If you don't like who you are, start TODAY making the appropriate changes until you become someone that you're proud of and that you would never want to change. Someone who YOU KNOW women want and love to be around.

# #4 THINKING GIVING HER APPROVAL GETS APPROVAL

Kissing women's asses in order to get approval in return is a completely unbalanced and inefficient approach to getting women to like you and it NEVER works unless there's something they already want from you. In that case, they're just using you and you're already on the losing side. They don't actually like you or feel attraction the way you think they do. They see you as a gullible and naive man they can get resources from.

When I was 15 years old and got my first job at Sea World, my dad, who I love dearly and has always been a terrific father, basically told me that in order not to get fired, I have to be the perfect employee and a "yes sir" kind of guy. That's the way he was because he was in the military for 20 years and grew up in a different time period than I did. Since I didn't know any better, I was usually afraid and timid that at any moment I could get fired so I, unknowingly, always kissed up to my supervisors and managers to make sure I was in good standing with them. You know what that got me? A lot of the opposite. During my first few jobs, my bosses were never close to me and never treated me like they liked me. I was treated like someone who annoyed them and they didn't like and I couldn't figure out why.

It all started making more sense when I worked as an Aircraft Mechanic at a place that did custom aircraft interiors under two older guys named Rick and Roger. To be blunt, Rick and Roger could be real assholes. They had the reputation of being hard to work for because they were both heavy drinkers, expected the job to be done right the first time, and had short tempers. They knew what they were doing, were very good at their jobs, and just didn't care about being polite or politically correct. Rick was a helicopter gunner in Vietnam and his life expectancy was something around 25 seconds so, after doing that crazy job for so long, he just quit giving a shit.

In my first two months there, Rick never spoke to me or in front of me. He just stared at me as if I was some dumbass from another planet. Roger spoke but was always short and to the point. No joking around or being friendly. After two months, I began approval seeking and telling Rick "good morning" and instead of telling me good morning in return, he would, literally, keep walking without acknowledging me. Eventually, about 2 months later, I told him "good morning" one last time and without looking at me or breaking stride he sarcastically asked, "What the fuck is so good about it?" and, as usual, kept walking. I thought, what's wrong with this guy! My co-worker said that's how he is - all business and doesn't care what you think about it. So, one Saturday morning after drinking heavily at the bar the night before with some co-workers, running on 2 hours of sleep, and still drunk and sobering up at work, which you should never do, I decided to break the ice. Knowing he wouldn't respond, I told him "good morning" and as he kept walking, I said, "Hey Rick. I have a question." He turned to me holding his usual cup of coffee in his shaky hand, tilted his head back, looked down at me as if I was nobody and asked, "Whatcha got?" Had I been sober, I probably wouldn't have done this but I asked, "How much longer before you go into a nursing home because I'm going to make it a lot sooner if you don't say good morning to me." Clearly, I was joking BUT he turned purple. Not red, but PURPLE. He didn't make a sound or move. He just gave me a death stare as he processed what just happened. He turned away, started walking, and waved his hand and said, "come on". My co-worker mouthed to me, "What the hell are you doing?!" At that point, I was sure I was fired. I followed him. We went out of the door in the back of the hangar, he told me to close the door all the way, and he just stood there watching the sun come up. He reached under his jacket, pulled out his cigarettes from his shirt pocket, handed one to me, put one in his mouth, lit it, and handed me the lighter. We stood there in silence for over 5 minutes while he held his cup of coffee in one hand and smoked his cigarette using the other. As he flicked his cigarette onto the tarmac and turned around, he walked right up to me, looked down at me, put his shaky finger in my face and, and with a half-smile, he said, "If you weren't a such little shit who liked to screw with me every day, you wouldn't have a job here. Remember that. Get back to work." From then on, he started telling ME good morning and asked me how everything was coming along! What?! The best part is that HE KNEW I was still drunk!

This happened because I decided to change my mindset from approval seeking to "I'm going to screw with this guy". What could have gone horribly wrong went over better than anticipated because instead of seeking his approval, I decided to do the opposite and poke the bear. On a side note, had I paid more attention in the first few months I worked there, I would've realized that ALL of the mechanics who kissed his ass, complemented him, bragged, and tried to build rapport with him got laid off or fired. He didn't want "bullshit artists" working for him. He didn't like people who kissed his ass. He wanted people who were straight up and didn't care about his approval. He didn't give approval unless you earned it and I respected him more than any boss I'd ever had before. Something about it drew me in and made me want to be a better employee.

As I pondered on this very risky lesson I learned, something occurred to me. I had NEVER met a woman who was as much of an asshole as Rick and if I could build a positive relationship with this Clint Eastwood type of guy who scared and intimidated most people he met, then surely I could build better and more effective relationships with women. From that moment on, a shift happened in my mind and I quit giving women approval in order to get theirs in return. I learned how completely unnecessary it was and it just didn't feel right to do it anymore. Instead, when I met women and interacted with them, I started behaving more like Rick. Not like an asshole, but as someone with the mindset of, "I know my personal value, I know what I bring to the table, I approve of myself, and I don't really need YOU to approve of me. I'm also not going to approve of you yet either because I don't know you. You're someone I don't know and me kissing YOUR ass would be completely insane. I need to learn who you are as a person FIRST so I can be sure you're someone who can add value to my life instead of being a problem. I need to be sure you're not some psycho who I will regret getting involved with."

Although this mindset sounds harsh and somewhat negative, it's a highly effective and realistic risk-management strategy that can and will save you A LOT of problems in your dating life. How many times have you met women, got overly excited, got emotionally involved too quickly, and it became a very problematic situation? How much of a headache did it turn out to be? I know I've done it dozens of times! It happens because we fail to think and have the mindset of, "What IF this woman isn't who I think she is and I'm only getting excited because she's pretty? What IF she doesn't have it together as much as she's making it seem she does and she's a real problem to be in a relationship with? What IF she's being totally fake with me right now? What IF she's a possible waste of my time?" How much differently would you behave around women with that mindset? How much more power would it give you in the moment? How would you respond differently than you normally do? Would you put ALL of your cards on the table or all of your eggs in one basket like you usually do and kiss the ass of a woman you know nothing about? Or would you SLOW DOWN and be smarter about it to sure she's a stable and well-rounded person before you embed her in your life and attach a bunch of relationship strings?

MOST MEN aren't wise, knowledgeable, or experienced enough to interact with women on this level and with this mindset, or they simply don't know any better, and they blend in with the herds of other men not getting dating life they want. They never stand out, get women's attention, or build deep attraction. They just think, "Oh my God I might get laid tonight!" and they jump in head first and get involved with someone they know NOTHING about.

**Problems with giving approval to get approval in return:**

- It's mentally and emotionally unstable to kiss up to someone you don't know just because you think they're physically attractive and they might touch your wiener.

- Giving someone a ton of approval THAT YOU DON'T KNOW lowers your social value and makes them think less of you.

- Giving someone tons of approval that you have zero information on and you know nothing about makes you look desperate, weak, needy, and insecure.

- It's not a challenge in any kind of way. You come off as way too easy and women find it boring. They're sick of guys throwing themselves at them and not making them work for it.

**Benefits of withholding approval and not giving it away freely:**

- It makes you more interesting. It adds mystery. It gives you more personal value. It communicates that your cup is already full, women are lining up to date you, you're not desperate to find a date or get laid, and you're seeing whether or not she meets the standards you set for the type of people you want in your life.

When women see they have to pass some sort of test or meet a standard to be in your life, the ones who are worth having in your life and actually make it better will rise up to the occasion and show you their worth. The ones who are a waste of time and like to play games will show you their lack of worth by complaining, making excuses, or walking away. Let me clear, as long as you have your own approval first, THERE IS NOTHING WRONG with making women earn your approval. There are too many fake and crazy women out there today with no sense of direction and that will waste your time. YOU HAVE TO have some kind of system to make sure they're up to par. Women are doing it to you every single day! What's wrong with making them play their own game? What's wrong with making them pass their own test? There's NOTHING wrong with it and it's important to fully believe it down to your core if you want to attract more and higher-quality women and improve your dating life.

- Women push HARDER to get your attention and you have MORE of their attention when you're giving them resistance and withholding approval. Push back and challenge them. Reality check - when you're giving away approval, not being a challenge, and women don't have to earn anything from you because your cup is completely empty, they're bored and actively looking to meet OTHER GUYS who aren't as boring.

- Withholding approval communicates you're a safer bet. That you're more stable because you're actually testing them and seeing who they really are. You're not gullible and taking their word at face value. Crazy men don't take such precautions.

- It communicates you're more mature, experienced, and you know what want and what you're doing. Most women pull away the minute you start kissing their ass BUT, when they sense you're not interested in kissing their ass at all, but rather, more interested in making sure they're not a waste of your time, the exact opposite happens. They become intrigued by you more than any man they've met in MONTHS and YEARS! Maybe even ever! This is NOT an exaggeration. This mindset is extremely rare and extremely powerful when done right.

Withholding approval IS NOT manipulation or game playing in any way. It's not being mean or cold-hearted. It's smart and effective and multiplies your dating success. It's a powerful strategy that saves you from looking and feeling like a moron and it keeps your precious time and energy from being wasted by women who aren't serious about you.

Freely giving away approval is a selfish rookie mistake and it makes you look weak and unattractive. It's crucial to APPROVE OF YOURSELF FIRST and make women and others prove their value to you. This doesn't mean you have to be a tyrant. It only means to stop being gullible and taking the sale too soon. Control your emotions and stop getting so excited because some woman is looking at you and giving you some attention.

Women are more committed to you when they have to work to gain your approval and trust. I'll say it again. WOMEN ARE MORE COMMITTED TO YOU when they actually have to make an investment, put some skin in the game, and have to work for your time and approval. She's not calling the guys giving their approval within the first 10 seconds, minutes, or hours. She's not sleeping with them. She's not dating them. She's calling, texting, sleeping with, dating, marrying, and popping out babies for the guy who has a lot of personal value and doesn't come off as desperate and needy. They guy who isn't making it way too easy and boring for her. The guy who's making it interesting and exciting and keeping her attention long term. The guy who's making her feel deep attraction.

# #5: THINKING YOU AREN'T GOOD ENOUGH FOR HER

I attracted A LOT more women when I started being good enough for MYSELF. That's the key. If you aren't good enough for yourself, you'll NEVER been good enough for women. This shit you see in the movies where the nerd who constantly feels sorry for himself gets the hottest girl in school isn't real and it'll NEVER happen to you. Quit fantasizing. In real life, that nerdy little dweeb would have to look himself in the mirror, decide to man the hell up, quit acting like a pitiful victim, and learn how to communicate more effectively with himself and those around him. He would have to change his self-beliefs and his habits, get under some iron to become physically bigger and stronger so he's not a scrawny twig, and educate himself on how women work. He'd also have to get his face out from in front of his phone, computer, and TV and read some books on how the world works and what skills he needs to develop in order to flourish in life. That's his only chance to make a serious transformation and land that cheerleader who all the football players are hoping to bang.

I've dated women who weren't good enough for themselves and, initially, I told them, "No. I'll never get tired of you. You are good enough for me. I love you. I don't understand why you see yourself that way and why you don't see what I see." You know what happened? I got sick of them. I got sick of their self-defeating, poor me, bullshit attitude and personality and it drove me absolutely nuts. I'm one of the nicest and most understanding people you'll ever meet but, even for me, that self-deprecating nonsense was way too much to handle and I eventually snapped and ran away. Day in and day out of someone needing you to validate them and make them feel better about themselves takes its toll and eventually, you want nothing to do with them. You don't even want to hear the sound of their whiny voice. It just becomes too much. Maybe you know someone like this and can relate to it.

The purpose of me talking trash about some women I've dated is to give you a glimpse into what women are thinking when you don't believe you're good enough for yourself or for them and they're better than you. It's annoying to them. It makes them want to slap you and shake you like Marlon Brando did to that one guy in The Godfather where he tells him, "You can act like a man! What's a matter with you?!"

Ok, so what if you ARE good enough for yourself but you still think she's out of your league? You can quit being so damn cruel to yourself already and figure out what you can do to improve to possibly be in her league. There are no excuses. Let's say you're overweight and she doesn't like fat guys. Is that her problem? Her loss? No! It's yours because you have the personal power to choose what you stuff into your fat face and you have the time and energy to exercise and get your body into a better condition. Maybe you're in that condition because you're always bullshitting yourself about what you're capable of doing. Stop doing that already! Get real with yourself, stop being weak, read some books and watch some videos on mental toughness and PUSH yourself to do better. You do have a choice and you can be good enough for her if you actually tried. Let's say you don't make enough money and you're broke as a joke. That's not society's fault. It's not the government. It's not "the man". THAT'S YOUR FAULT. Does it cost money to read a book? Nope. Does it cost money to watch financially educating videos on YouTube? Nope. Does it cost money to TRY to get a higher paying job? Nope. Does it cost money to open up Microsoft Word and write a book like this one? Nope. If you don't own a computer to go to a public library and do it. No excuse.

If you don't feel you're good enough for women, you have the power to at least DO SOMETHING about it to move in the right direction.

# #6: THINKING TELLING HER HOW YOU FEEL WILL DO THE TRICK

If there's one thing that has screwed up more potential relationships in my life it's telling women how I feel about them in order to make them feel more attraction or, even, fall in love with me. Look, when you don't know you don't know! But, if you do know and you keep doing it, you can't blame the women anymore and you can't blame your lack of knowledge or training. All you have to blame is yourself!

More times than I can remember, things would be going great with some girl I was getting to know, whether it was over the phone or in person, and  as soon as those emotions came up for me that told me I couldn't live without her, you know which ones I'm talking about, I want her as more than just a friend, and I couldn't stop thinking about how wonderful she is and I could spend the rest of my life with her, I felt the undeniable need to open my big fat mouth and tell her. My brain told me not to do it but the fact that not telling her about how I felt drove me absolutely insane motivated me to say at least something about it. Every single time it came up, my brain would tell me, "Marc, stop. Calm down. We've been here before. In this SAME EXACT POSITION and you opened your trap and ruined it! Don't do it again. Just wait it out and see what happens." You know what I said to myself, "Shut up, brain, I got it this time. I've thought about what I'm going to say word for word and it's going to work." I had done it dozens of times before, it never worked, and my train of thought was that she was just the wrong girl for me or I just didn't use the right words or phrases or voice tone. Hell, it also didn't help that my friends would tell me she wasn't the right girl for me either! Little did I know, I was being given the wrong information and the only reason they told me that was because they also didn't know any better!

Dozens of times and using dozens and dozens of approaches, I attempted to tell women I was getting to know how I felt about them as some sort of "next step" to progressing the relationship. IT NEVER WORKED! Not even one time! Had there been times when SHE said it first? Yes, and things went better. But, most of the time, I opened my mouth first and ruined it, like most of us do.

This quit happening when I changed my approach and the way I thought about it. I would rack my brain wondering why the women I didn't like were all over me and the women I did like didn't like me as much as the women I didn't like! The more I racked my brain, the more it started to make sense - I treat the women I don't like DIFFERENTLY than the ones I actually do like! But how? I thought about it more. Well, first, the women I don't like, I don't kiss up to them. Second, I don't ACT like I'm really into them. I'm just normal around them and I treat them the way I would anyone else. And last, I would NEVER in a million years actually say something to them to make them think I'm really into them. This pattern of behavior caused the women I didn't like to call me non-stop and invite me out with them all of the time whereas the women I actually did like NEVER did that. So, now that I figured out what I was doing, I had to figure out how to duplicate it with the women I actually did like TO SEE WHAT WOULD HAPPEN. I actually believed it wouldn't work AT ALL and they would think I was an asshole but, I was willing to take my chances.

With the next insanely attractive women I met that I was borderline obsessed with, I did the opposite of everything I actually wanted to do. Instead of telling her I wanted to "take her out", so cheesy, I invited her to hang out "with me" and told her if she can't, it's not a big deal. Did I really feel that way? Hell no! It was a major deal! I leaned away from her while I was driving instead of instinctively leaning towards her. I stayed completely calm and almost unimpressed when talking to her. I didn't' compliment her. I didn't give her a bunch of approval. I didn't treat her like she was special. At one point, she unintentionally touched my arm, apologized, and without skipping a beat, I wiped my arm and told her, "Yea, please don't do that again, gross." and I pretended to be an asshole about it. She laughed so hard that I had to wait 2 - 3 minutes for her to finish. When most women would be ready to go home, she suggested going to my place and watch a movie! I was shocked! But, instead of letting it show, I played it cool and said sure. While watching the movie, she fell asleep on my lap and hugged me while sleeping. I thought, "WHAT IS HAPPENING!?" When the movie ended, I took her home, made out with her in the car, put my hands in some awesome places I usually didn't get to touch on the first date, and went home in complete disbelief. You know what else happened? I dated her for 2 YEARS! She even insisted on going with me to another state when I had to move there for a job! What a powerful difference. Night and day. You know what else was different? I never told her how I "felt". Everything just "happened" on its own and there was no need to share my feelings. She understood what was happening without me opening my yapper.

Since then, I HAVE NEVER OPENED MY MOUTH AGAIN about how I feel and I've never had women run away because I didn't tell them how I feel. In fact, the opposite happens! Women tell ME how they feel and it happens so often that now it's just something I expect! My reality now is 100% DIFFERENT than it was then. Today, telling women how I feel about them is an absolutely insane idea and I wouldn't do it if you paid me to.

I have a rule about feelings that I've developed over the years and I use it in 100% of my friendships and relationships. I even made a video about it on YouTube. It's called the 50/50 Rule. One part of the rule is you NEVER reveal how you feel about someone if they haven't first communicated it to you. You NEVER tell a woman you like her if she hasn't said it first. You

NEVER, EVER tell a woman you love her if she hasn't said it first. If she doesn't use the words "I like you" or "I love you", then you don't either. Only mirror what she says. If she says, "I think you're a cool guy", you say, "Thanks. I think you're a cool girl." NEVER go past where she goes. EVER. It's important to mirror her output because what she's putting out is what she's comfortable getting back. You getting it? If you don't want to follow this advice, that's fine. It's only advice but I promise you this is the best possible approach to sharing your feelings with women. If she doesn't say anything and she's playing it cool, then you do the same.

Also, DO NOT try gauging where she's at by asking questions to see how she feels and seeing if she's hot and cold. LEAVE IT ALONE and just have a good time with her. Everything will fall into place on its own if you just don't poke at the subject. Nothing annoys women more than when things are going great and the guy makes it awkward by talking about feelings and "the next step" and "the next level". It's a total buzzkill and her mental boner for you goes limp almost immediately.

Forget talking about how you feel and if she says something first, NEVER REVEAL MORE THAN SHE DOES. It's OK to reveal less but you have to be balanced and know what you're doing. It's very easy to hurt her feelings and come off as the type of jerk women don't like. An example of this is if she tells me how much she enjoys spending time with me and she looks forward to seeing me more and spending more time with me, I'll crack a joke and say something like, "Thanks for the warning. I was hoping you wouldn't like me." If executed properly, she'll laugh, physically assault me by smacking me on the shoulder, and the attraction will continue piling up with the jokes, playfulness, and banter.

The golden rule is, if you still don't get it, keep your mouth shut about how you "feel". Even if it means not talking to her for a few days so you can get yourself in order. It's better than gushing and ruining everything.

# #7: THINKING ATTRACTION IS ALL ABOUT LOOKS AND MONEY

A guy I worked with, who will remain nameless, didn't have the best-looking face and definitely wasn't in good shape. To be even more specific, he is in his 30's and generously overweight. He doesn't really have any muscle tone and looks as if it's likely he'll have some significant health issues by the time he hits 50. He even walks like he isn't in the best shape and possibly having health issues. What makes this man unique is he attracts and dates hot, successful, and high-quality women. He's not rich or famous, not a doctor, definitely isn't an athlete, and could use improvements in the looks department. So, if this is the case, how does he do it? How does he attract these gorgeous, friendly, and marriage-material type women who are really into him? His personality and mindset. Whether it's something that comes natural to him or he's worked on it over the course of his lifetime, I don't know. It's not something I've ever brought up to him or discussed with him.

Let me tell you exactly what it is about his personality that makes him attractive to women. If you're not taking notes, you might want to do it here. This is something you want to glance back at from time to time. He's a very stoic guy who doesn't constantly express his emotions. He keeps a perfectly straight face most of the time. The word "stoic" means you're focused and all about handling your business. You don't believe in being a highly emotional and subjective type of person. The word "subjective" means adding emotion to something instead of just seeing it for what it is. On top of that, he doesn't run his mouth and freely express what's on his mind. He keeps a lot of things to himself unless they absolutely have to be said. If you ask him something personal, he doesn't hesitate to ask why you want to know.

When he looks at you, it's with no fear. He doesn't look at you like you're below him and he's better than you and he doesn't look at you like you're above him and you're better than him. It's clear that kind of stuff isn't important to him. He looks at you like you like it's only you and him and he's focused ONLY on what's going on between the two of you. Whether you're asking him to borrow a tool or you're having a serious conversation with him, he's locked in and giving you his full attention. That commands a lot of respect.

When he smiles, it usually isn't a full smile unless it's something really funny that really catches him by surprise. It's the type of half smile that says, "Ok. That's funny but I'm also busy and focused on other things." When he laughs, it's on his own terms. He doesn't do it to follow everyone else or because he feels obligated. He doesn't look around at other people to see if they're laughing or if he has their approval. It's because HE feels like laughing and doesn't care what you think about it. Also, when he laughs, he isn't out of control of his body. You know how when some people laugh, they're all over the place and moving around for no reason at all? Yeah, he doesn't do that. He stands still, looks you in your eyes, and laughs. He maintains that eye contact and connection with you. Very powerful.

When he isn't smiling or laughing, he keeps a straight and relaxed face. Not like the serious or wannabe tough guy who's consciously keeping a straight face and there's all this tension in his eyes and facial muscles. It's completely unconscious and natural. His eyes and facial muscles are relaxed and he's completely comfortable in his own skin. He'll even joke around with you and not even crack a smile but, you can tell by his tonality that he's only kidding and not trying to be an asshole.

When he moves, it's at HIS SPEED, not your speed. When he walks, it's at HIS SPEED, not your speed. HE SIMPLY DOESN'T CARE as much as the average guy. He's not fearful of something weird or embarrassing happening. He lives in his own reality and creates his own rules for himself. He consciously chooses his own thoughts and behavior regardless of what's happening around him.

Do you notice the significant difference between his behavior and personality compared to the average guy? You notice the differences between his behavior and personality and yours? What makes him so attractive to women is HE DOESN'T CHANGE HIS BEHAVIOR AROUND THEM. He's the same dude regardless of who he's around. He's not like the guys we know that behave one way in front of our friends and another way around women. He's consistent and not all over the map.

He is one of many men I know that aren't rich or famous and yet, they have no problem attracting women because of their powerful mindset.

Let's make this subject a little more complex. Although it's completely possible to attract women without being rich or famous, being rich and famous DOES help so you shouldn't completely eliminate the idea of making more money and being known for doing things with your life.

Dan Bilzerian is the guy you see on Instagram with all the insanely gorgeous women around him and who better to listen to about women and dating than guy who's, not only, surrounded by them 24/7 but sleeps with ALL of them? Most people think the guy is a total douchebag trust fund brat because they're jealous or they don't understand him but, if you actually watch some of the guy's interviews, you can easily see WHY women want to be around him. Observe how he carries himself and listen to him speak and you'll quickly realize he's insanely smart and has a lot of wisdom and insight into how women and the world work.

Something he said that stuck out to me was that even though you can attract women without money, fame, or being known for doing something big with your life, money, and notoriety multiplies your ability to attract women by 1000 times and makes it 1000 times easier.

This is important to wrap your mind around because a lot of guys are STUCK in the mindset and brainwashed to think that they can ONLY attract women by impressing them with money and wealth and if they can't get rich, famous, or look like a fitness model then they're doomed to dating average and mediocre women. Not true at all.

Another inaccurate and ineffective mindset is that women are ONLY attracted to money and beef cake guys. Again, guys only think this way because they're brainwashed by the internet, magazines, music videos, and social media. Not all women are shallow and looking to date men who look like models.

Let's expand your mind. If you had a low-paying job where you were constantly broke and you had to live a very limited lifestyle to survive or you had a high-paying job and your life was easier, which one would you take? Of course, you would take the one with more money. You know you would. So, why are women wrong for wanting to date a guy who can provide for them faster and easier over the guy who's broke but has a great personality? It's not a simple subject, is it? It's important to entertain both sides of the idea and develop a balanced perspective when it comes to money and women. Women aren't bad or wrong for not wanting to date the dude who lives in a cardboard box and they're not bad or wrong for wanting to date the guy who can more easily provide and give them an easier, more exciting, and more fulfilling life.

On the same note, being rich doesn't guarantee women will like you. They say money amplifies your personality and the more money you have, the harder you have to work on being a good guy who isn't a spoiled and self-centered tyrant. In the end, PERSONALITY is what truly attracts women and all other things are only added bonuses.

# #8: THINKING THE WORD "NO" WILL MAKE HER RUN AWAY

Being submissive and unable to say "no" to women is a MAJOR MISTAKE.

Think about the kids getting bullied who don't speak up for themselves, defend themselves, or say "no". The bullies see them as weaker and non-threatening and so they place a lower social status on them. If these kids actually stood up for themselves, talked back, and showed defiance, the bullies would lose interest and find someone weaker to pick on. Being weak and submissive doesn't make the bully want to be friends with the kid. It does the opposite and makes the bully severely dislike the person. Let me be clear, bullying is terrible and shouldn't happen but it does and I'm only attempting to explain some of the psychology behind it and how it relates to ordinary human behavior.

When women see you're weak and submissive and you don't stick up for yourself by saying "no" and expressing what you don't like and don't want, it triggers that "bully mentality" and causes them to lower your social standing with them. It causes them to, depending on their personality and moral compass, WANT TO USE YOU AND TAKE ADVANTAGE OF YOU because you have no borders and defenses.

If you can't say "no", not only, to women but to everyone else around you including your friends, family, parents, and kids, then you're opening up the floodgates and inviting trouble, misery, and failure into your life.

The word "no" is your first line of defense. A border you MUST use to protect your happiness and sanity. When women sense that border, they automatically feel more respect for you and they're less likely to bullshit you and play silly games. They're less likely to act like a bully with you.

# #9: THINKING SHE'LL FREAK OUT IF YOU GET PHYSICAL

I remember having lunch with this beautiful woman, whom I am still friends with, and sitting across the table from her being terrified and intimidated. She was calm, confident, pretty, she smelled good, the top of her smooth and tanned titties were hanging out and jiggling between her unzipped jacket, and I had convinced myself she wouldn't want me touching her in any kind of way. As if I was too dirty or not good-looking enough for her. I didn't think about the fact that she was having lunch with me, smiling, laughing, cracking jokes, and, from all appearances, enjoying herself. Over the next few weeks, she even invited me to her house to watch movies and drink wine. Each time I went, she was the same person, calm and having fun, and I was the scared little wuss terrified to attempt anything. One night, it was really late and she told me I could sleep there if I was too tired to drive home and invited me to "sleep" in her bedroom. You know what happened? NOTHING. I awkwardly laid there afraid to touch her until I fell asleep.

They say "the love hormone", Oxytocin, is at its highest level first thing in the morning and it definitely was when I woke up. Without thinking, I turned around, wrapped my arm around her waist, and pulled her in as close as possible. Again, the fear was GONE. I pushed my erection into the back of her shorts and NOTHING BAD HAPPENED! Then, I began to massage those lovely sweater stretchers under her bra and again, NOTHING BAD HAPPENED. Then I turned her around, started kissing her, and... you can figure out the rest on your own, you pervert.

The point is, I WAS AFRAID FOR NO REASON AT ALL! Yeah, this might not have been possible right after our first lunch but it became more and more obvious to me, through her behavior, what she was and wasn't comfortable with. She made it crystal clear!

From experience, if I notice she's having a good time, laughing, joking around, challenging me, making perverted jokes, unafraid to touch me and it appears genuine, 99% of the time, she has NO PROBLEM with me touching her or getting physical with her. In fact, I've noticed that when women are having a great time with you, THEY WANT that physical bond to begin as soon as possible! The sooner you initiate the physical contact, the more comfortable they'll feel! Brain studies have revealed that physical touch lights up the brain more than words and displays. Physical touch creates that powerful mental connection that overrides everything she may be thinking. If she's unsure of you, thinking it's too soon, or she just has a lot going on in her mind, initiating the physical connection overrides all of it. That space and unfamiliarity she senses between you and her gets eliminated and you and her INSTANTLY become closer.

So how do you know if it's OK to touch her in any way? Just pay attention to her behavior and responses and if you're not sure, just be cool and don't do anything. Eventually, every woman shows you in one way or another whether or not she wants to be touched. I mean, for goodness sakes, this woman invited me into her bedroom and I laid there with my hands crossed like I was in a coffin! So embarrassing...

Sometimes you just have to be brave and say "screw it" and see what happens. 60% of my success with women is from JUST DOING THAT and taking that chance of being wrong! I completely agree with Wayne Gretzky. He said, "You miss 100% of the shots you don't take."

A lot of women admire when you're brave and risky because it boosts their self-esteem and makes them feel better about themselves. It tells them they're the type of woman that a guy has to work up the courage to bridge that attraction gap. Being brave creates the fireworks that make the moment that much more intense and exciting. I've had women do it to me and it felt awesome and flattering so I can only imagine the way it makes women feel when they like you and you reciprocate those feelings through getting physical with them.

Something highly important that you need to remember is women can sense from a mile away when you're scared. Everything about your behavior and demeanor gives it away and being scared can actually HURT your chances of progressing the relationship. Some women are fine with you being afraid and they're more understanding about it but others may think you're too inexperienced or weak for them and it turns them completely off. Those legs slam shut and it becomes a desert down there. Instead of seeing that fur burger up close, it only becomes a mirage.

If you want to create and build tons of attraction, YOU CANNOT BE AFRAID OF WHAT WILL HAPPEN if you decide to get physical with her in any kind of way. You have to be mentally prepared for anything. You also can't be 100% locked in on it happening because if it doesn't, you'll be very disappointed. Have I had women tell me, "Wait. Stop. It's too soon."? Sure! It's happened A LOT. What did I do? I replied, "No problem. I don't want to make you uncomfortable." Then I backed off, told Mini Marc "down boy", and acted like it never happened.

If it's not the right time, too soon, or she, literally, doesn't want me touching her, which has happened, and it was super awkward, I don't get butthurt or make things weird. In my mind, it really isn't a big deal. I don't make it worse by getting upset and making her uncomfortable.

On a final note, when you're afraid to get physical because you're afraid she may disapprove, you're placing yourself beneath her. That is the last thing she wants. NO WOMAN is attracted to any man who's beneath her and needing her approval and validation. The more often you practice getting physical, the easier it gets and the more you know what to do.

THE BEST DATING TIPS, HELP, & SOLUTIONS – MAJORLEAGUEDATING.COM

# #10: THINKING SHE THINKS THE WAY YOU DO

I saved the worst for last because this is what I believe to be the biggest thing stopping you from creating, building, and maintaining deep and real attraction with women. It's also a very common mistake when people are put in a position of leadership because they expect people to just KNOW what they're thinking.

The men who are having the worst "luck" with women and failing in their dating life are doing so because they're either confused or upset about women not behaving and responding the way they EXPECT them to. They're confused and upset that women aren't behaving and responding the way THEY do. This is solely from a lack of experience and education.

Before I decided to do whatever it took to turn my dating life around and develop the ability to attract women faster and easier, I used to always think, "Well, if I were her, this is what I would do. So, I don't understand why she didn't do that! She SHOULD be responding to me in this way and I'm upset AT HER because she isn't!" The problem was I was only thinking like MYSELF and failing to realize that women are completely different. I failed to realize that not everyone is exactly like me and they don't think, respond, and feel the same way about things as I do. It may sound pretty cut and dry right now but how many times have you become frustrated with or at someone because they weren't doing the things YOU wanted them to do or doing them the way YOU wanted them done? Exactly. You failed to slow down and consider that not everyone thinks the same way you do and you may have to step into their shoes to understand them better to see what they're seeing and feel what they're feeling. You failed to realize that not everyone operates the way you do.

The problem with wanting, wishing, and simple-mindedly believing women SHOULD think, respond, and feel the way you do is that you're setting yourself up for failure through closed-mindedness and ignorance. Getting upset because women aren't behaving like you and responding in the way you would respond is a costly mistake. When you're saying the sky should be purple because that's what color YOU see and you're upset because everyone else is saying it's blue, you're spinning your wheels, working against yourself, and not making any progress in any direction.

If you ever find yourself struggling with this problem, the most important thing to do is to put your pride and ego away and forget about yourself for a while. Forget about your beliefs, insights, and the way YOU believe the world works and SHOULD work and only focus on understanding other people better. Start seeing things from their point of view. Start learning about how they feel about certain situations and topics and why they feel that way. Start observing women and making mental notes on the way they respond and behave and the things they choose to talk about. It may not make sense at first but the more you do it, the more it will make sense and the easier it'll become to get the results you actually want. This is extremely important to do because if you're getting bad results with women, you're upset that they're not functioning the way you want them to, and you actually believe THEY'RE the ones with the problem, it means you're so locked into your mindset and belief system and you have such a big ego problem that you're completely blinded to what's really going on. You're completely blinded to the way the world ACTUALLY works vs. how you THINK it works.

If you can get over yourself, learn how women actually work by paying more attention to them than you do yourself, and then adjusting your mindset and behavior to match what you've learned, I guarantee you will have 5 to 10 times more dating success than you're currently having.

# PART 2: A DEEPER LOOK INTO ATTRACTION

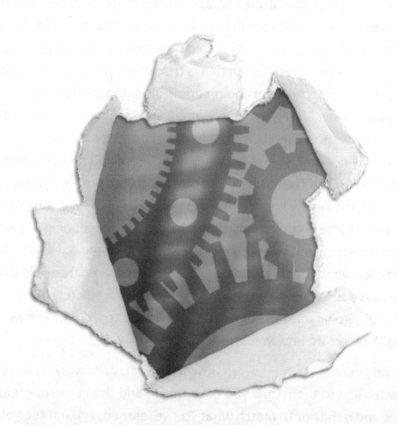

# PERSONAL MAGNETISM

OK, let's get weird. Magnetism is a quantum, or very small, property that can be grown and amplified from something as small as an atom.

Magnets generate invisible and outward extending magnetic fields and when other similar magnetic fields are within range, they automatically attract eachother. These magnetic fields are generated by electrons and, to make it simple, electrons congregate in "shells" around the nucleus of an atom. The magnetic ends of electrons in a "filled" shell point in opposite directions, work against eachother, and cancel eachother out - making the shell of the atom non-magnetic. But, the magnetic ends of electrons in a "half-filled" shell all work together. Instead of pointing in opposite directions and cancelling out each other's potential power, they all point in the same direction and work as a team to create magnetism. Even though they're more independent of eachother than the electrons in a "filled" shell, they're all on the same page and doing the same job to reach the same goal.

When it comes to attracting, dating, and keeping women around, if your mind and life are in constant disagreement, confusion, and misdirection, you destroy your personal magnetism. Instead of a generating a strong inner power easily felt by all women you interact with, you radiate conflict, weakness, and insecurity. Women sense something is "off" about you. But, when your mind and life are both on the same page and focused on the same goals, your personal magnetism is amplified.

Pretend your mind is the nucleus of an atom, your thoughts, emotions, words, behavior, and habits are the electrons floating around it, and the magnetic ends, or purposes, of those electrons are all pointed toward specific goals, results, and outcomes. Together, this structure makes up your mindset, how you conduct yourself, and the results you're getting.

THE BEST DATING TIPS, HELP, & SOLUTIONS – MAJORLEAGUEDATING.COM

## Non-Magnetic Atom

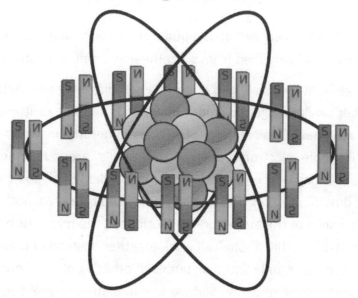

## Magnetic Atom

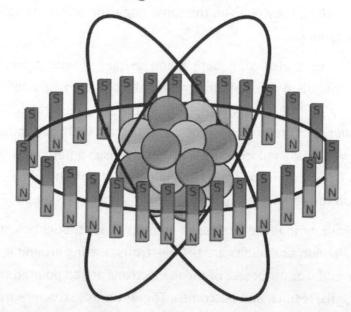

Magnetic and Non-Magnetic Atoms © Major League Dating

## The "Filled" Mind

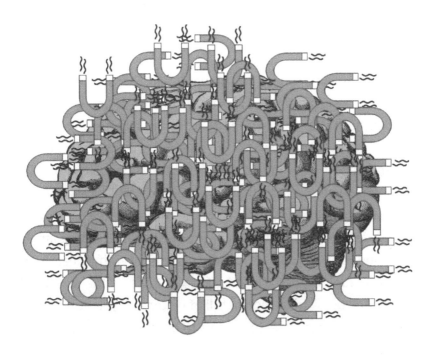

The Non-Magnetic Mind © Major League Dating

Just like a "filled" shell of an atom sabotages its own magnetic capabilities, a "filled mind" sabotages personal magnetism and makes attracting women into your life more difficult and frustrating. Your mind lacks the correct "magnetic" structure to pique women's interest and make them feel pulled in and drawn to you. Your thoughts, emotions, words, behavior, and habits are twisted, tangled up, chaotic, without purpose, and on different pages. Your mental, emotional, and behavioral incongruencies cancel out and ruin your personal magnetism. It's clear you're not exactly sure of what you want, what you're looking for, and where you're headed. It's clear your life is chaotic, without order, and being pulled in several different directions.

Instead of your mind being an organized, powerful, and magnetic tool you use to pull whatever and whomever you want into your life, it's a collection of random and useless information - and your life and results reflect every ounce of it.

A "filled" mind is like a sponge full of water and breeds the perspective and attitude of a closed-minded, "smarter than you" know-it-all. Without any strategic hesitation or consideration, you're highly prejudiced, opinionated, biased, and closed off to anything that can potentially improve and benefit your mindset and life. You leave no room to learn, grow, develop, evolve, and become. The impenetrable wall around your mind with no doors leaves you stuck in the past and incapable of progression and reform. Eventually, your personal and dating life easily resemble modern-day Cuba - an outdated country with a dilapidated infrastructure due to being "closed off" to so much of the world. What happens when you fill up a sponge full of water and you don't rinse it out or get rid of the excess water? It begins to breed bacteria, mildew, and it stinks! It ruins the sponge! If your mind is that sponge and it's always full of old water, your mind begins to stink and rot. A rotten and stale mind definitely doesn't attract the right people, women, and opportunities into your life and it definitely doesn't make you appealing.

A "filled" mind causes you to stumble, trip, fall, and crawl through your dating life with one problem after another and, since you know it all, you're smarter than everyone else, and incapable of accepting and processing feedback and constructive criticism, you blame everyone but yourself for the constant and reoccurring problems you experience with women.

Rather than being the magnetic person that pulls women in and keeps them around, your "filled mind" pushes everyone and everything away and makes you more egotistical, ignorant, and ineffective.

## The "Half-Filled" Mind

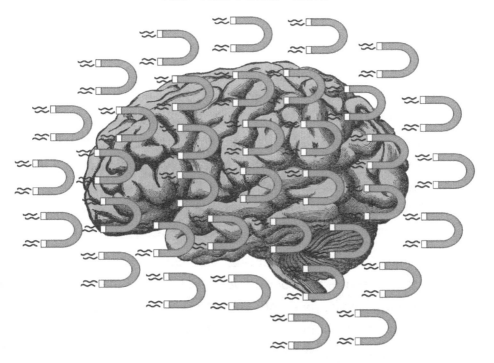

The Magnetic Mind © Major League Dating

When your mind resembles the atom with a "half-filled" shell, it's almost inevitable that women like you, feel compelled to interact with you, and are uncontrollably "drawn" to you like a magnet.

Your thoughts, emotions, words, behavior, and habits are clear, concise, organized, congruent, intentional, purposeful, and strategically directed at specific goals, results, and outcomes. You have a better idea of who you are, what you want, and where you're headed. You're more humble, open-minded, and flexible. You lose the need for unfounded and unprovable biases and opinions and proactively eliminate random, useless, ineffective, unnecessary, and unattractive thinking, emotions, mindsets, and behavior to make room for improvement.

Because a "filled" mind blocks your ability to absorb, you refuse to be a know-it-all. You're willing to listen, learn, and accept the painfully obvious reasons behind the failures and lack of results in your personal and dating life. This, along with seeking wisdom, knowledge, and improvement, gives your thoughts, emotions, and behavior, or your inner magnetic ends, purpose. They're forced to "align" and focus on the goals and desired outcomes you want most. When everything happening in your mind is for a reason and serves the same purpose, your personal magnetism becomes powerful enough to "pull" whatever and whomever you want into your life with less effort. The force your inner power creates does the work for you. Your personal magnetism creates the deep and intoxicating "attraction" women desperately want to feel.

Once you understand this basic concept of personal magnetism, eliminate the nonsense, and your thoughts, emotions, and behavior all serve a specific purpose, your inner power and personal magnetism become too strong for women to resist. When the attraction begins pulling them in, they're powerless. Friends, family, co-workers, and associates trying to pull her away and "protect" her doesn't change her mind about you. The force your inner power and personal magnetism generates keeps her "snapping", like a magnet, back into your life.

When you don't understand the concept of personal magnetism, it's like turning the same two magnets around. Instead of feeling "pulled" to you, women are pushed away. The magnetic fields no longer match. Without making a change to one of the magnets, regardless of what you do, they will NEVER snap together. The force keeping them apart is as strong as the force that binds them. Convincing her to like you, buying flowers and dinner, and telling her how much you like her doesn't change your mind's magnetic structure or the attraction she feels. To create powerful attraction with women, you must turn yourself into a powerful magnet.

# WOMEN'S BRAIN STRUCTURE

When it comes to the differences in men and women's perception and behavior, some stereotypes do seem to be supported by research.

To examine and study the human brain in 1901, scientists completely removed it from the cadaver and weighed, poked and prodded, dissected it, and did a bunch of freaky deaky stuff to it. Today, we use more advanced and less-invasive methods to examine the brain's composition, structures, and relation to behavior. But, regardless of the methods used to examine the brain, one consistent finding throughout time is that the hippocampus, part of the limbic system, is larger in women's brains.

## The Female Limbic System

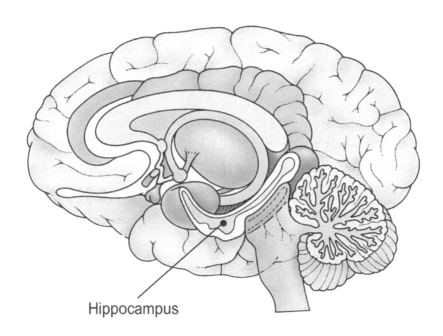

Hippocampus

The Female Limbic System © Major League Dating

The hippocampus, an important part of the limbic system, the region that processes and regulates emotions, is sensitive to the female hormone, estrogen, and grows faster and larger in women. Researchers and scientists believe the larger hippocampus explains why many, if not most, women respond more strongly to emotion than logic and why they, a lot of the time, socially outperform men. Because of the larger hippocampus, women feel a wider and deeper range of emotions than men and they're more in touch and expressive with their emotions and feelings. The larger hippocampus also provides the increased ability to bond and feel connected to others. This explains why women hug more, go to the bathroom together like weirdos, are the primary caretakers for children, and why there is no society on earth where men assume this role.

If you have a hard time understanding women and attraction, what they want, and why they respond and behave the way they do, the larger hippocampus is your first clue. It makes a big difference in how she thinks, feels, responds, and determines what she wants in a man, for herself, and for her life. If you expect women to think and reason the way you do, then it'd be wise to begin shifting your thinking and awareness.

Although research continues to reveal other structural differences in men's and women's brains that affect perception and behavior, I believe the hippocampus difference is the most important one because you'll encounter and contend with this difference on a regular basis. It's 99% likely to be reason for friction, conflict, and disagreements with women.

Awareness of women's superior ability to feel and process emotion and why they do it is your first step to understanding women and attraction on a higher level. The difference isn't just in her background, upbringing, education, religion, or perception and understanding of the world. It's also in the structure of her brain and how it processes and relays incoming and existing information.

# MEN ARE MORE LOGICAL

## Men's Brain

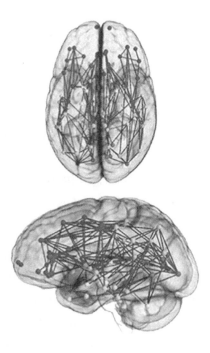

Male brain neurological map from the National Academy of Science/PA

There is no single definitive and correct answer when it comes to male and female behavior and the how those differences relate to differences in male and female brain structure. Not yet, at least. It's an ongoing debate between scientists and researchers and will continue to be for decades to come.

The overly-simplistic theory and generalization that men are left-brained and purely logical and women are right-brained and purely emotional is a highly reported misconception continually driven by those refusing to dig deeper into the subject. That being said, my observations and extensive experience with women and dating have taught me there might be a degree of truth behind this theory and generalization. Men aren't completely left-brained and purely logical and women aren't completely right-brained and purely emotional but we, as men, do naturally tend to lean more towards logic and women naturally tend to lean more towards emotion. It's a complementary match. Although never true 100% of the time, it's a pattern you'll definitely notice, if you haven't already.

The human brain is made of two cerebral hemispheres - the left and the right. The left hemisphere is, theoretically, responsible for analytic thought, facts, logic, language, linear thinking, reasoning, science, math, writing, and numbers skills and the right hemisphere is theoretically responsible for feelings, art, creativity, imagination, intuition, insight, music, and spirituality.

In December 2013, Penn Medicine researchers discovered definite differences, not in brain structure possibly associated with behavioral differences between men and women, but in neural connections or "wiring". Based on gender, major intra- and inter- connective differences were found in the left and right hemispheres of both the cerebrum and the cerebellum. Intra- means inside. The "intranet" doesn't import or export data in and out of the system. Only back and forth. Inter- means between and among - "internet" transmits data in and out of the system.

In males, greater neural connectivity was found from font to back within each hemisphere suggesting men's brains may be structured to facilitate greater connectivity between perception and coordinated action. In other words, the intraneural connectivity from front to back, but remaining in the same hemisphere of the brain, explains why it's easier for men to remain calm, logical, clear, sharp, and precise, and free of emotion for longer periods of time when we're using the left side of our brain and why we're able to become so highly emotional, addicted, and obsessed when we're using the right side of our brain. No matter which side we're on, we tend to move back and forth in that one side without jumping back and forth between the left and right hemispheres. Whatever logic or feeling we're experiencing, we're more likely to stay in that "zone" for longer periods of time and it's harder to snap us out of it.

These findings support marriage expert and comedian Mark Gungor's take on how men's and women's brains work in his DVD special "Laugh Your Way to a Better Marriage". He says, "Now men's brains are very unique. Men's brains are made up of little boxes and we have a box for everything. We got a box for the car. We got a box for the money. We got a box for the job. We got a box for you. We got a box for the kids. We got a box for your mother somewhere in the basement. We got boxes everywhere! And the rule is, the boxes don't touch! When a man discusses a particular subject, we go to that particular box, pull that box out, open the box, and discuss ONLY WHAT IS IN THAT BOX!, and then we close the box and put it away being very, very careful not to touch any other boxes." Although he's making a joke of men's thinking and behavior, he couldn't be closer to the truth.

When I'm doing something really logical, like writing this book, and my girlfriend comes in starts going off about something that's happening at work or with friends, I'm really not interested in listening or engaging in conversation with her. She loves it when I get like that by the way. Not. I'm in my "book" box. I don't care about ANYTHING happening outside of what I'm doing until I'm done. My mind is in the zone and I only want to go back and forth in the part of my brain that I'm using. When I'm done, I mentally detach from it and then ask my girlfriend, "What did you say earlier about the person with the thing?" Then she, of course, gets upset that I wasn't listening and I never listen, lol. Great times.

# WOMEN ARE MORE EMOTIONAL

## Women's Brain

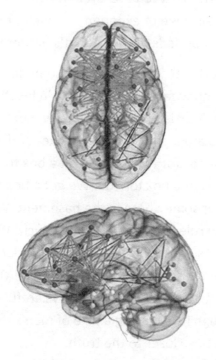

Female brain neurological map from the National Academy of Science/PA

In the same DVD special "Laugh Your Way to a Better Marriage", Mark Gungor says, "Now, women's brains are very, very different from men's brains. Women's brains are made up of a big ball of wire and everything is connected to everything. The money is connected to the car, the car is connected to your job and your kids are connected to your mother and everything's connected to everything. It's like the internet superhighway and it's all driven by energy that we call 'emotion'. It's one of the reasons that women tend to remember EVERYTHING. If you take an event and you connect it to an emotion, it burns in your memory and you can remember it forever. The same thing happens for men. It just doesn't happen very often because, quite frankly, we don't care. Women tend to care about EVERYTHING!"

It's interesting Mr. Gungor came to this conclusion 10 years before the Penn Medicine study because it appears his comical theory is supported.

While men's brains are more "intraconnected" between left and right hemispheres, meaning that they don't constantly jump back and forth between the two, women's brains are more "interconnected". They constantly jump back and forth between hemispheres in both the cerebrum and cerebellum. Since connectivity is greater BETWEEN the left and right hemispheres, it facilitates communication between analytical and intuitive - meaning women can switch between logical to emotional quicker and with a lot less effort.

Like Mr. Gungor said, when we're in our mental "box", we stay in that box. Women, on the other hand, connect everything to everything and, from the National Academy of Science's neurological map of the female brain, this is easily apparent. It explains why so many women can go from calm to emotional and "crazy" before you can figure out what's happening!

The results of the 521 female and 428 male brain scans suggest male brains appear to be better optimized for the logical application such as high-pressure competitive mathematical and logistical environments and spatial awareness and female brains appear to be better optimized for more emotional application such as intuitive thinking and verbal skills.

Before anyone gets their undies in a bunch, this is not a "sweeping generalization" about men and women, their brain structure, neural connectivity, or their thinking and behavior. It's a connection of my own observations of men and women using brain and neurological studies. In the everyday world we live in, the majority of men display behavior highly indicative of a more logical mind and the majority of women display behavior indicative of a more emotional mind.

As a man, you're more likely to come to answers and conclusions using logic. You naturally do what's logical, rational, and what makes the most sense. You don't dig deep to see how you "feel" about it. You find what makes the most sense and you roll with it. Women, on the other hand, are more likely to come to answers and conclusions using emotion. They're more likely to naturally do what their emotions and intuition tell them to do. They actually DO dig deep to see how they "feel" about it!

When it comes to attracting women, most of us attempt to get women to like us by doing what's "logical" and makes perfect sense. Things WE, if we were in her shoes, would quickly respond to. We figure if it makes sense to us, then it "should" make sense to her and work! BUT remember, 90% of the time, women's minds don't work "logically" like ours do. They don't always respond to the things that make perfect sense to us. They're spending more time being emotional and "feeling" things while we're not taking ANY of that into consideration when we're coming up with our "foolproof" strategy to attract women.

# THE 10% – 15% DIFFERENCE

The data on men's and women's brains isn't to suggest that men and women are 100% different in thinking, behaving, and responding. They're not. My interactions with women, including short-term and long-term relationships and, even, living with them for years at a time have revealed that 85% - 90% of our thoughts, behavior, reactions, likes, and dislikes are extremely similar and, for the most part, have very little to no impact on attraction. The purpose is to suggest that the 10% - 15% difference between the male and female mind is where attraction is actually affected. It's where we find A LOT more success with women.

When women consider you a "stranger" because they don't know you, there's an invisible, instinctive, and yet, real, "wall" that exists between the two of you. It's not there because of the 85% - 90% of commonalities you, her, and most people share. She's comfortable with that. It's there because of the 10% - 15% difference between you, her, and every other person. The 10% - 15% that makes up your unique individuality and personality. She doesn't know that part of you and making assumptions, on her part, is dangerous and can lead to her wasting her time on you. So, behind that "wall" is her attraction button and in order to locate it and pound it so she feels the emotion and attraction you want her to feel, it's important to focus on the area where she keeps it - the 10% - 15% separation between you and her.

You can point out the 85% - 90% of commonalities you and her share all day long and, at best, it'll only catch her some of her attention and make her think you're a "nice" guy. But, it won't cause the wall to come down. Her attraction button is NO WHERE NEAR the area most guys prefer to poke around. It's not where you discover the both of you like pizza, dogs, and walks in the park. It's NO WHERE NEAR the area where you discover the both of you like certain types of music, social media pages, or activities. She can easily find these general commonalities with most men but it doesn't guarantee she'll feel attraction for any of them.

Never make a big deal about the 85% - 90% of things you have in common with women. Avoid bringing them up and keep it short if she brings them up. 99% of guys make it a goal to seek out and pinpoint general commonalities with women and it gets them nowhere. When you develop the "it's no big deal" mindset about the 85% - 90% of the things you have in common with women, it's much easier to break through or climb over her "wall" and get to her attraction button.

This 10% - 15% difference between the male and female mind is where attraction lives. Where it escalates rapidly and your wildest dreams come true. Where you're pounding on her attraction button so hard that she works up the nerve to touch you, kiss you, or grabs you and tells you you're coming home with her.

When you meet women, before you open your mouth to sell yourself and say what she's likely heard other men say, stop, think about, and focus on the 10% - 15% that actually makes the two of you different.

There are two ways to do this. The first is to ask questions, be a good listener, and observe heavily. Seek to learn and understand the differences. Observe and learn how much more emotional, cautious, and hesitant she is and why. Observe her natural responses, listen to her words, the way she says them, and seek to understand the thoughts and reasoning behind her facial expressions, gestures, movements, and responses. From this you'll quickly learn what makes her feel safe, comfortable, happy, and what bothers her. Most men focus on the 85% - 90% instead of taking the time to "get" her and truly understand her as an individual. When she sees you understand this, the wall begins to come down and the attraction button is quickly revealed.

The second is to consistently conduct yourself in a way that communicates you're more aware, different from other men, and understand attraction better. That you know and avoid the mistakes most men make with women and how they make women feel. A way that communicates the 10% - 15% she doesn't know about you is interesting, attractive, and far from ignorant, sketchy, creepy, or weird.

You communicate this through your posture, composure, attitude, mood, facial expressions and the way you walk, talk, move, look at her, touch her, and speak to her. Every little thing you say and do and the way it's said and done conveys information that she's constantly collecting and processing. When her eyes begin to squint while she's listening, it's happening. When she says, "Oh really... wow that's awesome!", it's happening. The more she likes what she sees and hears, the more the wall comes down and the easier it is to access her attraction button and pound on it. Slam that button like you're on American Ninja Warrior.

Both approaches used simultaneously work best. Since all women are different, feel them out to see which approach gets the best response. Some women respond better to the first, some better to the second, but most, respond well to both.

As you can imagine, both approaches take practice, repetition, and reflection. Practice the first. With other women, practice the second and throw in some of the first. Then repeat over and over and over with every single person you meet. After each interaction, make it an unconscious habit to replay everything in your mind. Reflect on what you said and did that was good or bad, the positive and negative responses you received, how those responses made you feel, and learn from all of it.

You won't get it right the first time. These are skills developed through trial and error and over time by meeting and interacting with one woman after another. The more women you interact with, the better you get.

# PART 3: MAKING THE MENTAL SHIFT

# THE IMPORTANT MENTAL SHIFT

More success with women means opening your mind, making a permanent mental shift, and never going back to your inexperienced, ineffective, and amateur mindset. It's designing your thinking, behavior, and responses around what you understand about the way women's minds work. It's understanding the real 10% - 15% difference, why she, and other women, won't always respond the way you expect or want them to, and being totally OK with it at all times. It's becoming more flexible in your mindset and choosing not waste energy being upset about women not responding the way you think they SHOULD.

Designing your thinking, behavior, and responses doesn't mean being fake to make women like you. It means knowing and understanding exactly which behaviors, thought patterns, and responses build and destroy attraction and having enough self-control to limit yourself to saying and doing only the things that you know will hit her attraction button.

Making this important mental shift means becoming more calculating in your thinking and reasoning. You go from the mindset of "because I would respond THIS way, she should respond the same way" to "since I have a better understanding of her mindset and the way she thinks and feels, is this particular thing going to freak her out? How will it make her feel? How many other men have, probably, said and done this exact thing to her? How would other women respond to it? Will it damage or help the attraction I'm trying to build?"

The sharper and more focused you become in your thinking and reasoning, the more you sharpen your mental sword and the better you become at spotting crucial opportunities to build attraction instead of letting them pass you up.

# LIKING ISN'T ATTRACTION

Men who struggle to attract women make the rookie mistake of thinking "liking" and "attraction" are the same. They're not. Her liking you is much different from her feeling attraction and wanting you as more than a friend. She can like you but not have feelings of love or companionship for you. She can like you and still not be comfortable with you invading her personal space and touching her, kissing her, or getting physical with her. She can like you but still not want you sexually.

Liking is a detached and objective state of mind. She's thinking, "He seems cool and I don't mind him as long as he doesn't do anything weird or make me uncomfortable." Feeling attraction, on the other hand, is an attached and subjective state of mind. She's thinking, "I hope he likes me and I hope I don't say or do anything that makes me look weird and unattractive."

When she only likes you, she's stoic and unemotional about it. She's not figuring out how to make herself more attractive so you'll want her. When she's feeling attraction, she's more emotional about it. Her mindset is attached to the idea of being more than a friend. She's toying with the idea of potential love and companionship with you.

Most relationships begin at liking and quickly escalate to attraction, but not always. You'll meet women who, for some reason or another, won't like you as a person but still want a sexual relationship with you.

Focus on attraction instead of getting women to like you. Convincing her you're a nice and great guy is a waste of time because most women automatically like you anyways when they're feeling attraction. When she's feeling attraction, her powerful emotions automatically override any logic you were trying to use in the first place.

# WOMEN DON'T THINK ATTRACTION

A big reason you struggle to spark attraction is because, again, you believe women think and respond the way you do. You attempt to extract logical responses from women instead of emotional.

Women don't "think" attraction. They feel it. They don't take time outs and convince themselves to feel attraction because you're nice, funny, and considerate. It can't be conjured up or planned. It's not an on/off switch she has access to. Only you have access to it - something we'll cover later. Attraction just happens and the moment it's sparked, she feels it and she's completely aware of it. It hits her like a sledgehammer.

Doing things women don't naturally respond to creates a HUGE disconnect and makes sparking attraction all the more difficult. The wall around her attraction button becomes stronger and higher. Things women don't naturally respond to is anything boring, too logical, and not emotionally stimulating. Examples are buying gifts, giving her money, paying bills, over-complimenting her, kissing her ass, putting her on a pedestal, giving too much approval, convincing her how much you like her, and calling and texting too much to show her what a nice guy you are. Things to "show" her what kind of guy you are don't spark attraction because you're attempting to manipulate her into the logical mindset of "thinking" instead of the emotional mindset of "feeling".

The more experience you get with women and the more you understand which thought patterns, behaviors, habits, and responses trigger emotion instead of logic, the easier it becomes to spark attraction with women you meet. It becomes so easy, in fact, that it's second nature - like a new language you become fluent in.

# SHE CAN DISLIKE YOU AND STILL FEEL ATTRACTION

I stated before in this book that sometimes you'll meet women who, for some reason or another, won't like you as a person but still want a sexual relationship with you. This is because the logical part of her mind dislikes you because you're too different, you pissed her off, or you annoyed her, but the emotional part of her mind is still triggered, curious, and seeking excitement. In that moment, you're, logically, repulsive yet, at the same time, emotionally stimulating. It sounds crazy but it happens.

She can hate your guts BUT if she's feeling emotion when she thinks of you, it can create intense feelings of attraction she can't turn off. On the other hand, if, when she thinks of you, her mind goes to a cold, callus, and purely logical place, your chances of her feeling attraction for you are zero.

It's extremely common for a scorned woman, from an emotional mindset, to talk passionately about how much she hates a certain guy. The truth is, she's so passionate about it because she can't stop thinking about him. Even though she doesn't "like" him as a person because of whatever he did or didn't do, she's still attracted to him and the logical and emotional conflict is driving her crazy. As much as she wants to, she can't turn the attraction off!

Think about this - her being pissed at you is far better than her thinking you're a "really nice guy". "Pissed" is emotional. "Nice" is logical. At least, when she's pissed, she's associating emotion with you. The "feelings" are triggering her to see you as more than a friend, be sexually attracted to you, and to think about you non-stop. "Liking" you because you're "nice" doesn't put her in the same mindset or you in the same position.

# TRIGGERING EMOTION MATTERS

I also stated earlier in this book that when she's feeling attraction, her powerful emotions override the logic happening in her mind. They override both the logic you were strategically using to build attraction, like trying to convince her of how great of a guy you are, and the logic SHE was using to "protect" herself. By protect herself, I mean that the average woman, who doesn't know you but notices you're easily likable, as soon as she's caught off guard by the sudden jolt of attraction and the feelings associated with it, and in an attempt to snap out of it and regain some self-control, a logical dialogue takes place in her mind. Just like the movies, a little devil appears on one shoulder and a little angel on the other. Part of her says, "Screw it. Let's do it. I'm curious. Who cares if you just met this guy? He's awesome! You only live once. Let loose and see what happens!" The other part says, "No, don't do that. Be cool. Don't be crazy. Don't embarrass yourself. Don't make him think you're a slut. It's way too soon to feel this way about a guy you don't know. This could be a mistake. You should back off." When the attraction is sparked and emotion is taking over, the logical reasoning and dialogue taking place in her mind becomes less important than what she feels. All of a sudden, she doesn't care if she doesn't know you. Your face, age, height, weight, financial status, and friends aren't as important anymore. The way you're making her "feel" becomes more important than anything else. When you trigger the powerful emotion, logic makes its exit.

Women gush about the man they want, but 99% take the one who stirs emotion. Not the tall, handsome, muscular guy with piercing eyes, but the one who triggers emotion, sparks attraction, and keeps it going. TRIGGERING EMOTION IS THE KEY TO ATTRACTION. The sooner you trigger emotion, the sooner she feels the powerful attraction.

# EMOTIONS GUIDE HER ACTIONS

Because emotions and feelings override EVERYTHING she thinks she wants, she can quickly and easily go from out of your league to in your league in a matter of minutes. Very few women can resist the effect emotions have on them and once you stir up emotion, access her attraction button, and pound on it, she's powerless. The emotion puts her in a trance and overrides all logic and logical decision-making. Her emotions are boss and she does what they say. This is great news if you're stirring up a lot of emotion and she's feeling a lot of attraction but terrible news if the emotion isn't there and the attraction is dying.

Remember, her brain doesn't work logically the way yours does and her actions are heavily guided by the emotions she's feeling. They're influencing her thoughts, decisions and reactions. She's processing information, behaving, and reacting based on what she "feels". Logic is not playing a major role in anything happening in her mind.

She also doesn't control WHAT stimulates her emotionally. Just like she can't choose whether or not to be attracted to you, she can't choose what she does and doesn't find emotionally stimulating. It doesn't matter if you're not the nicest guy or you have a terrible credit score, when the emotions come up and the attraction is sparked, she feels it. It rises up from the pit of her stomach and floods her entire body. From there, in her mild to heavy state of confusion, anxiety, excitement, and giddiness, she can choose to act on it, give it time and let it fester, or, if she has a high degree of self-control, walk away. She can choose what to do about the emotions she's feeling but she can't turn them off or force them to disappear.

When you notice the objective to subjective mindset shift happening, it means you're headed in the right direction.

# PART 4:
# ATTRACTION
# POWER

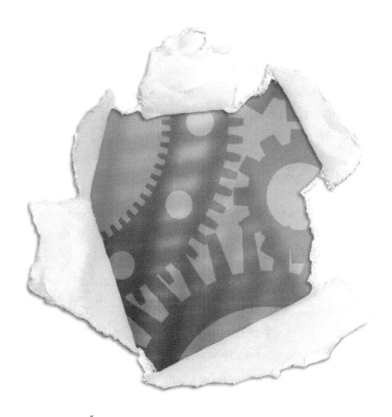

# YOU CONTROL HOW SHE FEELS

When she's feeling emotion that's continually transformed into deep and heavy attraction, she's powerless because she doesn't control the process. She's doesn't control your words and actions that stir up her emotions. She's doesn't control how that emotion becomes attraction. She's doesn't control how much that attraction grows. ONLY YOU DO. When the emotions are stirred and she's feeling attraction, YOU ARE IN CONTROL. Since you intentionally created the attraction in the first place, you control it. She can't turn it off or dial it down.

It's the same as when a girl you like shows a lot of interest in you, gets you excited, and then vanishes or starts ignoring you. You're not in control of how you feel about her. It drives you crazy and you can't turn it off! SHE made you like her and got you worked up. SHE created the emotion and the attraction you're feeling. ONLY SHE can decide what to do with it now. The amazing power this girl has over you is the same exact power you have over any woman who's feeling emotion and attraction for you.

Friends can't talk her out of it and family can't convince her not to feel the way she feels. She can't even talk herself out of it! When you've created the emotion, sparked the attraction, and pounded on her attraction button, NOT EVEN YOU can talk her out of it! When you turn your mind into a powerful magnet, she can't resist the "pull" you create.

With this power comes great maturity and responsibility. In this highly-emotional state, women are very weak, naive, and gullible. They're trusting you and expecting you to be good to them. It means not playing with women's emotions to boost your self-esteem. It means not making women fall in love with you so you can use them for sex, money, etc. This is mental and emotional abuse and I am 100% against it.

# SHE WILL GIVE YOU HER POWER

### Attraction Power

### Rejection Power

Attraction Power vs. Rejection Power © Major League Dating

THE BEST DATING TIPS, HELP, & SOLUTIONS – MAJORLEAGUEDATING.COM

When building attraction, it's important to understand the constant balance of power between you and women. Biologically, she needs the power to protect herself. She uses it to feel safe and weed out weak men who aren't likely to produce strong and healthy offspring. You, on the other hand, need the power to attract women. You use it for inner strength, to stir emotion, and to maximize your chances of "spreading your seed".

Picture the "power" as a glowing ball of energy that women, by default, already have and we, as men, don't. Women already have it because, in the human mating process, as well as the mating process of many other species, the female is the prize. Males pursue, females get pursued, and men, unconsciously, want the power women have over them. Take, for example, the type of woman you consider to be untouchable and "out of your league". You can feel the enormous power she has over you when you talk to her. That's why you feel fear, nervousness, anxiety, and hesitation. It's like being on one of those singing competition TV shows - you do your little song and dance hoping she likes you and at any second, she can slam her hand down on a big red button, alarms blare, red lights flash, and your chances with her are over. In that moment, you're on her stage, she has the big red rejection button, and you can feel she has most, if not all, of the power and you don't. It's very intimidating. At the same time and with that same woman, think about how that power begins to move in your direction when you have her attention and she's interested. When she agrees to hang out or go on a date with you, you feel some of that power move in your direction and your confidence rises. Then, when she kisses you, you feel, even more, of that power come your way. Again, your confidence and self-esteem rise. Then, when things get hot and heavy and she feels safe and comfortable enough to sleep with you, you feel another MASSIVE transfer of power. That's why, afterwards, you feel amazing. Like a Greek God. Like nothing can ruin your incredible feeling of power.

When you feel the power moving in your direction, you're developing "attraction power". Attraction power puts you in the driver's seat. The more attraction power you have and if you use it correctly, the easier it is to keep her attention, stir emotion, and make her want you and fall in love with you. When she has all of the power and you have very little to none, like when you first meet her, she has "rejection power" and she can use it to make men she doesn't like go away. Rejection power doesn't make her mean, stuck up, or snobby. It makes her a woman doing what she's, biologically, meant to do - which is protect herself and weed out weak men who aren't likely to produce strong and healthy children.

Just to be clear, when the power transfers from her to you, its nature doesn't change. Only its purpose changes. When she has the power, it's used for protection. When you have it, it's used to attract. I can use a wrench to tighten a bolt or I can use the same wrench to break a window or assault someone. The wrench doesn't change. Only its purpose does.

Here's something else that's important to understand - when she feels the transfer of power happening and she's comfortable with it, she has you under a microscope. She's watching to see how you handle the power you've received so far. She has to trust you with it. If you get cocky, arrogant, and controlling, she shuts the transfer down because you're showing her not mature enough to handle it and it makes her uncomfortable. If you get weird, clingy, needy, and emotionally weak and confess your love for her, again, she shuts the transfer down. The weak and emotional display is too much, too soon. BUT, if you're relaxed and cool about everything and don't make a big deal about it, she will remain cool and relaxed as well and the transfer of power will continue. The point is, when we feel things are going great, sometimes we risk getting too excited and making mistakes. No matter how amazing it feels, always do your best to play it cool, remain balanced, and not become extreme.

What most men don't know or understand about this power and women's relationship with it is THEY WANT YOU TO HAVE IT! Most women are looking to get rid of the power they have over men because it's a burden. They don't benefit from rejecting men and remaining single. All they're looking for is the right man to come along, take the power and the burden, and then, in turn, use it to make them happy and fulfilled. Simply put, all women want a strong man in their life they can be submissive to and vulnerable with. They want to relax, let their guard down, be happy, and know the man they gave their power to will use it to protect them, love them, and make them feel secure.

As I'm sure you've figured out by now, for there to be any transfer of power, SHE HAS TO FEEL ATTRACTION. You have to stir emotion. She has to feel "pulled" in your direction. If you're boring, bland, and uninteresting or you display weak and unattractive behavior, the power stagnates and she eventually uses it to escape the interaction.

If she IS feeling attraction, how soon the transfer of power takes place depends on, both, you and her. It can start happening in 5 minutes or it can take weeks and months. If you're very experienced with women, you understand their thoughts and emotions, you're very good at communicating, and you know how to hold and conduct yourself in an attractive manner, then you'll notice it usually doesn't long for the power transfer to begin. If you're still learning and haven't experienced a lot of success and failure with women, which is vital to getting better, the process will usually take longer because you're going to be figuring it out as you go. At the same time, the speed of the process also depends on the woman. The more experienced she is with men, the more rejection power she's likely to have and the more protective of the power she usually is. She's been there, done it, and seen it. She knows the game. She's seen the tricks. She's familiar with the shortcuts and manipulation men use to get her power. She also knows she can have her way with most men and get anything she wants from them. On the other hand, if she's naïve and inexperienced and hands over all of her rejection power within the first week, you want to move forward with caution. Handing over power without hesitation is a red flag of a weak, insecure, and clingy woman who will make your life difficult. The type of woman you should take seriously is the one who is balanced and lets the transfer of power happen slowly as you prove you can be trusted with it. Every situation is different but the more women you interact with, the more patterns you'll notice. The more familiar you get with those patterns, the more likely you are to know what to say and do in those situations to get her rejection power out of the equation as soon as possible.

## Attraction Power / Rejection Power Balance

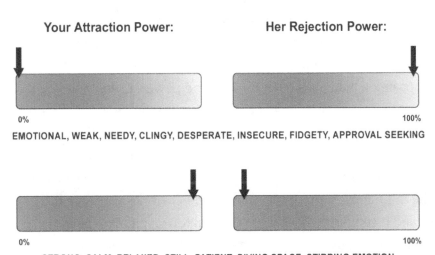

Your Attraction Power:

Her Rejection Power:

0%          100%

EMOTIONAL, WEAK, NEEDY, CLINGY, DESPERATE, INSECURE, FIDGETY, APPROVAL SEEKING

0%          100%

STRONG, CALM, RELAXED, STILL, PATIENT, GIVING SPACE, STIRRING EMOTION

The Power Balance © Major League Dating

From my experience, I've noticed the attraction power and rejection power work in perfect balance. They're harmonious. The yin and the yang. The power can move, both, in a positive and negative direction. When you stir emotion, spark attraction, and she likes the way you make her feel, she allows some of her rejection power to transfer to you and you gain attraction power. At the same time, you can inadvertently give the some or all of the attraction power back and it will inevitably and automatically return to its original form - rejection power. Think about the relationships you've been in that failed because you became weak, needy, and insecure. Everything was perfect and then one day you noticed the relationship taking a bad turn. Instead of remaining calm, cool, and collect and being smart about how you responded to the situation, you let your thinking and behavior change in a desperate attempt to save it. You acted nicer than you usually would and became insecure, unsure of yourself, and emotionally weak. You did weak and approval-seeking things you wouldn't normally do like kissing her ass more often and becoming her servant. Every single time you were too nice and physically and emotionally weak, you gave back some of the power. Every single time you put her on a pedestal she didn't need or want to be on, you gave back some of the power. Every time you failed to conduct yourself in a strong and attractive manner, you gave her back some of the power. The more it happened, the more of the power you gave back until, eventually, it was gone. When you had all of the power and were smart enough to conduct yourself appropriately so you'd keep it, she felt happy, safe, comfortable, and in love. As you gave the power back and it converted back to its original form, rejection power, she felt less and less happy, safe, comfortable, and in love. The rejection power you gave back through your ill-thought-out conduct took over and influenced her mind so much that she reverted back to the same biological state she was in when she met you. She felt she needed to protect herself and find a strong man who can give her strong and healthy offspring.

It's OK to lose a little bit of power here and there. It happens in all relationships. A small amount of the power bounces back and forth as you get to know her, in disagreements, and during the course of the relationship. But, it's important to see when your attraction power is leaking out through holes in your mindset, behavior, and habits. To see when she's losing attraction for you through tiny, and seemingly unnoticeable, reactions and behaviors. Identify which thoughts, reactions, and behaviors, are causing or contributing to the leak, educate yourself on how to fix the problem, as you're doing right now, and immediately make all necessary changes to patch up the hole and prevent it from happening again in the future.

From now on, with ANY woman you meet, keep in mind that the more power she senses the has over you, the more likely she is to remain in a logical state of mind and keep the power to herself. The power only begins to move when you get her out of that logical state of mind and into an emotional one. It only begins to move when she's feeling instead of thinking. It only begins to move when you're not giving your power away and fueling her rejection power through weak-minded thinking and behavior. When you make it obvious that it's easy to have power over you, it's like pushing a boulder up a mountain. No matter how hard you push to get to the top, the weight of your thoughts, actions, and habits around her will weigh you down and make it much harder than necessary.

This is a game of power. Do not make it easy for women to reject you. The goal is to quickly strip them of their rejection power and use that same power to spark, build, and amplify as much attraction as much as you can. When done right, women will thank you for it.

# SHE DOESN'T WANT YOU TO GIVE THE POWER BACK

Something else that will set you apart from other men and that women will thank you for is not giving the rejection power back. Again, it's a burden for women to have it and the only benefit they get from it is protecting themselves from weak and clueless guys who don't get it. But, this is not what any woman wants from you or any other man long-term. They're looking for you to understand how it works. To come into their life, take the rejection power away, and then use it in a responsible and positive manner to make them "feel" happy, safe, secure, relaxed, comfortable, and, at the same time, submissive and vulnerable.

There's nothing more frustrating, conflicting, disappointing, and heartbreaking to women than feeling a lot of attraction for you and you just don't get it. They're willing to take a chance and let you have all of their rejection power and instead of using it to make them feel, even more, attraction, you squander the opportunity. It looks as if you're deliberately trying to give it back! If they really do like you and feel, at least some, attraction for you, it's a very heartbreaking experience when you don't turn out to be the man they're hoping you are and that they desperately want you to be.

Remember, when the transfer of power happens, she's on your side. She's rooting for you. Every fiber of her being is hoping you know what you're doing with that power and you don't give it back. No happy woman in her right mind actually wants to go back to being single, having to protect herself from sketchy men, and worried about if and when she'll meet the right guy. She's looking for a man who understands the process and knows what he's doing throughout it.

Be the guy she's looking for. Stop taking the power you have to attract women and GIVING IT BACK! Stop focusing on making her "like" you and focus on stirring emotion and attracting her. When you're not doing all of the "logical" things other men are doing like being overly nice and needy and clingy, kissing her ass, seeking approval, putting her on a pedestal, over complimenting her, calling and texting too much, sharing your feelings, and bragging, she will give you her power and let you keep it.

Keep in mind, she can't take your attraction power from you. She can't force you to give it back. The only person in control of the flow of power is YOU. The only person who can give the power back is you. You only lose your attraction power when you think and behave in weak and unattractive ways. You're giving your attraction power back when you're trying to make her "like" you rather than causing her to feel attraction for you. You're giving your attraction power back when you're trying to make her "think" instead of making her "feel".

Don't make the naïve, clueless, and rookie mistake of thinking it "logically" makes sense to give her your attraction power in exchange for love, attention, and approval. Don't be dumb enough to believe she'll appreciate you and feel attraction for you because you were nice enough to let her have power over you. No matter how bad things get or how desperate you are, giving her your attraction power DOES NOT MAKE IT BETTER.

The worst part about giving the power back is she doesn't think you made a simple mistake that she can forgive you for and move on from. SHE RESENTS YOU FOR IT! She STAYS angry at you for it and it's a deep, hurtful, and unsettling anger. She's angry you lacked the ability to take the situation, friendship, or relationship and create something positive and memorable from it. As a consequence, she feels repulsed, confused, and like she can NEVER forgive you for being so dumb and clueless.

# KEEPING THE POWER FOR YOURSELF KEEPS HER FEELING ATTRACTION

If it isn't clear yet, which it should be, if you want women to constantly and continually feel deep and powerful attraction for you, it's important to strip them of their rejection power and use it to make everything go in your favor.

Stop giving away your attraction power by getting upset and frustrated when something isn't going your way. Stop giving away your attraction power by allowing the way you "feel" about her to overcome you to the point where you become overly emotional and you open your mouth and tell her you're in love with her and how she's the "one". Stop giving away your attraction power by kissing her ass and doing whatever it takes to get her approval, affection, and love. Stop giving away your attraction power by sacrificing and trading a real connection with her for a superficial display of who you think she wants you to be. In other words, stop ruining your chances with women by showing off, bragging, and drastically altering your personality in hopes that it will impress women and spark attraction. Stop giving away your attraction power by doing what's "logical" what makes sense to YOU.

Learn how women's minds work and how they think, feel, respond, and behave and why. Once you have a better understanding of attraction power and you quit making the mistake of assuming that all women do or should think and respond the way you do, the right things to say and do with women will present themselves and become more evident in the moment. A PERMANENT shift will happen in your mind, you will automatically think and respond in a more effective manner, and you'll never be able to return to your old way of thinking. Once the shift occurs, everything "clicks" and makes better sense, and you're attracting more women and with less effort, it will be impossible for your mind to revert back to its old ways. You've created a major shift and change in your reality. You've written over old information. You've reprogrammed your belief system with new evidence and facts. You've completely removed ineffective thinking patterns that were, at best, speculation, and you've replaced them with absolute "seen it work with my own eyes" facts and truth.

The simplest way I can explain the concept of keeping your attraction is power and not giving it back to her is by telling you to ALWAYS REMAIN CALM AND COOL NO MATTER WHAT IS HAPPENING. The man who can remain calm around women has the best chance with them. It doesn't matter if it's relationship issues, you lost your job, someone in your family is sick, your business is tanking, you totaled your vehicle, etc. The man with the most attraction power is the one with the most self-discipline and who can best control himself and his mind. The one who best controls his attitude and how he allows internal and external events to affect him. Now, don't fool yourself, THIS IS NOT EASY but it works better than words can describe. The man giving all of his power away is the one freaking out internally and externally all of the time. He gets flustered and upset because she's not texting back right away. He gets upset because she cancelled the date. He gets irritated because she won't say how she "feels" about him. He gets bent out of shape because he hasn't heard from her in a few days.

One of the biggest contributors to my success with women is I spend lots of time working on my ability to keep my emotions and in check and NEVER let it show when something is bothering me or driving me nuts.

# PART 5: POWERFUL MINDSETS THAT SPARK AND KEEP ATTRACTION

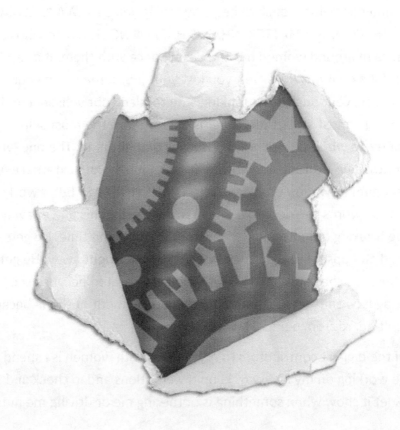

# ALWAYS KEEP IN MIND THAT WOMEN ARE SKEPTICAL

It's important to stop making the foolish mistake of assuming women are stupid and you can pull the wool over their eyes or pull a fast one on them. The guys constantly failing and putting themselves in terrible situations with women are the ones lying, manipulating, exaggerating, doing shady things, and actually believing they're smarter than everyone! They're failing to consider she's been involved with other men and it's likely she's seen and heard the lies and exaggerations before.

My dating life drastically changed when I set a strict standard for my mind and behavior and decided that I was going to be straight up with EVERYONE - my parents, siblings, friends, co-workers, bosses, strangers, all the way to the women I met and dated. I decided that I would stop ALL of the nonsense and be completely straightforward even if it didn't put me in the best possible position. That I would find a way to make things work from my newfound stance of never compromising my integrity for gain. That I would stop bending the truth, exaggerating, and not being 100% forward with people just to get ahead or get what I wanted.

After listening to one woman after another tell me how full of crap the guys they met were and how they wished more men would just quit bullshitting them and being fake, I figured there was something valuable to what they were venting about. That they weren't just empty complaints. That there was more to their expressions of frustration and being fed up with how they didn't understand why more men just couldn't be honest and direct. On top of that, they made it sound as if the guy should have nothing to be afraid of and how weak and wimpy they were for not having the balls to be more honest and transparent!

So, I figured if this is what women are honestly looking for and they're this passionate about it, I'm going to change my mindset and give it a shot. I'm going to experiment with giving women what they're asking for and see what happens.

From then on, I made sure to be straightforward as much as possible and, no matter how hard it was, I was as honest as I could be with women instead of saying things that made me look good. When they asked how many women I've slept with, instead of making up a number I knew was a lie and more socially acceptable, I gave a more honest estimate or an "I don't know" - because I honestly have no idea. When they asked what my intentions were, instead of the same lame answer that most guys give of "I want to get to know you and see where things go", I'd face them, look them in the eyes, and say, "I'm definitely interested in having sex with you because you're extremely attractive, I'm a guy, and being around you makes me pretty horny." What do you think happened? Women got mad and ran off? Slapped me? Threw a drink in my face? NONE OF IT HAPPENED! In fact, women locked eyes with me harder, squinted, even laughed, and 90% of the time, we had sex within 24 hours of me being completely honest about what I wanted.

Here's what most guys don't get - YOU ARE MORE TRUSTWORTHY WHEN YOU DON'T APPEAR TO BE TOO PERFECT. If your answers are too cliché and perfect, women assume you're full of shit. But, if your answers catch her off guard and surprise her, she AUTOMATICALLY begins to trust you and feel closer to you. You AUTOMATICALLY stand out and catch her attention because, even though, she may not be the biggest fan of what you're saying, she's a huge fan of your ability to take the risk and be honest. It builds massive trust, respect, and attraction and you stand head and shoulders above the rest of the guys she's used to meeting and dealing with. Become more transparent and It'll do wonders.

# #1: I AM THE PRIZE

A powerful mindset that dramatically improved my dating life was I quit believing that women were superior to me because they were pretty, popular, or had something I wanted. I quit believing I had to kiss up to them and get their approval in order to get what I wanted in return and, instead, I started believing I had something THEY wanted. Something rarer and more valuable than what they were able to give to me. Something rarer and more valuable than what OTHER MEN could offer. I didn't only believe it; I took massive action to turn MYSELF into that rare person all women are looking for. Into that man they struggle to meet and keep around. The man women will give anything to have in their life.

Let me be clear, seeing yourself as the prize in no way means you're a cocky, conceited, and arrogant asshole. It doesn't mean you believe you're superior to women and better than them. It doesn't mean they're below you. When you see yourself as the prize, you still respect women as people and intelligent beings. You see and treat them as equals. The only difference is you refuse to believe that women are somehow above you and you have to bow down to them like most men do

When you're the prize, you thoroughly believe that what you bring to the table is 10X more valuable than what the average person does. Since you have what other people want, you prefer for women and others to prove TO YOU that they're worth your time and they can add value to your life. You don't go out of your way to prove yourself to others so you can live in their reality; they have to prove themselves TO YOU because YOU KNOW that your reality is much stronger than theirs. You know you're stronger-minded, getting better results, and you're on a much better path than everyone else. You know you're a highly effective person, you stand out from the rest, and you can add tons of value to her life.

When you're the prize, you are a valuable man who's spent more time and energy than the average person working on his mind, body, and life and you refuse to accept ANYTHING mediocre or below-average in your life. You'll be damned if you're going to be desperate and lazy in your dating life and wind up with anyone who makes you unhappy, unfulfilled, and doesn't add value to your life. You've set personal standards for how you conduct and treat yourself and if you have to follow the rules, so does anyone else who wants to be part of your life. NO EXEPTIONS. NO EXCUSES. NO FREE PASSES. It doesn't matter who it is, what they look like, or their status in life. They have to rise up to meet your expectations.

You're the prize because you add value to yourself DAILY and your selection process ensures that NO ONE is using you or robbing you of your personal value. That no one is wasting your time and stealing your peace of mind and happiness. Your time, peace of mind, and happiness come first because they are the most valuable things in your life. I'll repeat this because it's critical for you wrap your mind around it and fully understand it - the most valuable tools you have to attract women, separate yourself from everyone else, and make yourself a highly valuable person are not your Rolex watch, car, house, expensive suits and shoes, or your Funko POP! collection. They are your time, peace of mind, and your happiness and you should fiercely protect them at all times. When you don't protect them and make them a priority, you will quickly notice your personal value and the way you feel about yourself take a nosedive and you'll wake up one day wondering what the hell happened, why your life sucks, and why you're not happy.

When you're the prize, you communicate that even though she may be beautiful and charming and all the guys want to sleep with her and marry her, you have just as much value and impact as her and you're not the easiest guy to get until she proves what kind of value she will add to your life. You communicate you'll never lower your standards or disrespect yourself by bowing down and worshipping someone you just met and barely even know. Even though she can usually snap her fingers and have any guy she wants, she can't do it with you. You're not a dog and you won't roll over just because she has a little treat in her panties. Before you become overly impressed with her, she has to demonstrate the value she ACTUALLY brings to the table through her actions, how she treats you, and how she behaves around you. A bubbly personality, pretty face, nice tits, and a nice ass will only get her so far. If her looks and fluttering eyelashes do it for you and that's what makes you lay down and surrender, then I have terrible news for you. YOU WILL NEVER be able to successfully incorporate and demonstrate the "I am the prize" mindset and you will fail to effectively communicate your personal value and reap the incredible rewards it brings.

There's nothing wrong with believing you're the prize and demonstrating it. There's nothing abusive or manipulative about it. Like other mindsets, it helps you weed out the bullshit and protect your time, energy, and investment in yourself. It helps you protect your personal value and prevent yourself from being sucked into friendships and relationships with the wrong people.

For the "I am the prize" mindset to work, you HAVE TO stop being desperate and gullible and you have to put massive action behind becoming the ideal you. The type of man who stands out from the rest and doesn't settle or give in as easily. A man with higher standards, higher expectations, and pushes himself harder. A man who protects what's important to him and expects everyone wanting to be in his life to offer value. When you're the prize, you're building a treasure for yourself inside your mind and you can't let just anyone near it. You have to learn what they're about, what their intentions are, and what they offer.

# #2: MY PURPOSE, GOALS, AND OPPORTUNITES COME FIRST

Men who sacrifice their purpose and opportunities in life to chase women will NEVER have the success OR WOMEN they want. The men who chase their purpose and take full advantage of opportunities will have more than enough success and just as many women wanting to be with them. In other words, if you chase women instead of success, you'll have neither and if you chase success instead of women, you'll never run out of either. Whatever package the lesson comes in, it's important to understand that you'll chase women away if you focus too much on having them and squander life opportunities if you neglect them and fail to take action.

From my time chasing women vs. chasing my goals, I've learned this to be 100% true. If you spend too much time and energy focusing on women instead of putting action behind bettering yourself, your life, and your career, you will end up broke and with someone who's a waste of your time. "If I can meet the right woman first and have her by my side to support me, then I can take over the world!" WRONG MINDSET. It RARELY ever works. Too many men, just like you, were on the right track, focused on the right things, taking action, making good progress towards a powerful and successful life, and then they met a woman who had a lot of power over them. The power she had caused them to neglect their goals and aspirations and instead, focus on making HER happy and giving her what SHE wants. They quit putting themselves and their life first, they abandoned their goals and aspirations, and before they know it, they were 65-years-old, divorced 3 times, and BROKE. They never got the life they actually wanted and instead, they struggled to survive in an unplanned, difficult, and chaotic life that HAPPENED as a result of losing focus and neglecting their purpose and opportunities. It happened so slowly they barely noticed it and so fast that it was too late to recover. Every year it was, "I'll get back on track soon. I'll do that thing I've always wanted to do here real soon. I have big plans to make my comeback here soon." Every single year it was the same thing until it was too late.

The more effective mindset, one that'll make you happier, is, "Instead of spending my time and energy chasing women, which I'll have time to do LATER, I'm going to focus MORE on reaching goals and getting myself and my life together RIGHT NOW. When I get to my destination, then I'll take a break from it and spend some time looking for the right woman." Realistically, when your life is on the right track and you're having a lot of success, you won't have to "chase" women because they'll be chasing you. They'll be beating your door down hoping you'll give them a chance.

The majority of successful men who have a great life spent most, if not all, of their time focused on chasing their purpose and opportunities. Their wife, or whatever women they're with, usually came into their life AFTER they were successful and it's ALWAYS someone they would have never landed if they were unsuccessful and focused on the wrong things.

Focusing on your purpose and opportunities above all else puts you into a powerful position to attract higher-quality women and who add more value to your life. It also makes you more valuable because most of the guys women meet are only focused on getting off of work, drinking beer, smoking weed, playing video games, and doing "easy" things that don't make them better.

I AM NOT saying you can't have a girlfriend or be married. I'm only saying to be smart about it and NEVER make the deadly mistake of making your relationship more important than your goals, opportunities, and purpose. The more success you have in life, the more valuable you make yourself. The more you neglect your purpose, the more you lower your value.

THE BEST DATING TIPS, HELP, & SOLUTIONS – MAJORLEAGUEDATING.COM

# #3: MY HAPPINESS COMES FIRST

Too many men are overly concerned with putting women's happiness before their own and it's creating major problems in their dating, love, and ENTIRE life. Yes, it's important to do your best not to take away from the happiness and comfort of the other person in any kind of relationship but when that same relationship starts taking away from your own happiness, comfort, value, and self-worth, that's where you draw the line. When you're not as happy or comfortable as you could be but you stay with that person or in that situation anyways, you're only devaluing yourself and robbing yourself of potential and attractiveness. You're allowing your mind to be filled with anger, frustration, and anxiety rather than peace and calm. Yes, I said "allowing" because you DO have control over it!

Whenever a person or situation causes me to think and say, "Nah, I'm not dealing with this dumb nonsense", I do WHATEVER IS NECESSARY to separate myself from that person or that situation as soon as possible. Some people believe life is too short to run away from everything that doesn't make them happy and if you continually run, you'll die lonely and miserable. I believe life is too short to waste your valuable time on ANYTHING that doesn't make you as happy as you want to be. That if you only spend your valuable time on the people and things that make you happy and ignore what doesn't, you WILL have a far more fulfilling life than most people have. Look, most people are too scared to run away from what doesn't make them happy and towards what does and that's why most people, deep down, don't feel truly satisfied. They're depressed and suicidal. They feel like they're cheating themselves and being unfair to themselves. They're staying in lame relationships so they're not "single", in marriages only for the "kids" and for tax purposes, at jobs they hate because they're afraid of change, hanging out with friends they can't stand so they'll have company, and the list goes on. When your happiness is more important to you than "comfort" and status, you'll go through whatever pain is necessary to feel happier. You'll do what you have to do to fix the situation and make it better. You won't find lame excuses to stay and to keep dealing with it. You'll make whatever needs to happen, happen. That's mental toughness. Mental strength. The kind of mental toughness and strength that EASILY separates you from weaker and less attractive men.

The man who understands his time on earth is limited and he has the courage and intelligence to put HIS own happiness first stands out like a "sore freakin' thumb", as my former boss, Don, put it. When you put your own happiness first, it's obvious in your personality and the way you carry yourself. You're more authentic and real instead of fake and saying and doing what you think people want you to say and do. You have an air of confidence that says "I won't accept or put up with dumb shit or anything that makes me unhappy." Not only is putting your own happiness first very intimidating to people who don't respect others' time, people who ARE A COMPLETE WASTE OF YOUR TIME, but it's also extremely attractive to women. It tells them you're serious about your life and what you want and you won't accept anything less. This mindset gets her juices flowing and makes her want to ride you like she's trying to get Robitussin out of there. That's a Chris Rock joke, by the way.

When your happiness comes first, you don't care how women feel about it or the comments they make to get under your skin. You recognize and understand that OTHER PEOPLE ARE RESPONSIBLE FOR THEIR OWN HAPPINESS and if they're not making THEMSELVES happy, IT'S THEIR PROBLEM AND NOT YOURS. It doesn't matter how hot she is, how nice she is, or anything else about her. IT'S NOT YOUR JOB TO MAKE HER

HAPPY. She has a brain, the ability to read and absorb information, and the ability to figure out how to make herself happier. If she's too dumb to figure it out then, I assure you, you're wasting your time and, in the long run, she'll rob you of your peace of mind and happiness. There's nothing worse than dating weak and insecure women who want everyone to make them happy instead of making themselves happy.

The men who are the most attractive to women are the ones who aren't ashamed or apologetic about putting their happiness first. The men not wasting their precious time on people and things that distract them and rob them of their value and peace of mind. The men not afraid to speak up for themselves and tell women to knock it off or they're going to be single. The men unafraid to walk away from a relationship and be single for as long as it takes to meet someone who makes them happier.

When your happiness comes first, you simply don't give a shit. I don't know how else to phrase it. It doesn't matter how hot she is, how beautiful her eyes are, how sexy her accent is, how good she is in bed, how much money her family has, or how much she spoils you, or anything else. You are willing to let it all go because you know the happiness and peace of mind that comes with not having to deal with her nonsense greatly outweighs any sort of comfort you feel being with her.

I've walked away from DOZENS of relationships with beautiful women who most guys would marry in a heartbeat because the headache of staying with them was worse than the headache of being single and looking. MY HAPPINESS COMES FIRST and if I'm not as happy as I could be because of the standards I set for myself and my life, then I am perfectly happy to let her go and let her be another man's problem. Again, LIFE IS TOO SHORT not to be happy and once you get your standards and values in order, you'll quickly realize how much nonsense is out there in the world and you'll do whatever is necessary to protect yourself from it.

# #4: IT'S NOT AS BIG OF A DEAL AS MOST PEOPLE MAKE IT

In my book **Declare War on Yourself - How to Get Your Act and Life Together to Become the Best Version of Yourself**, I talk about how most people aren't getting the results they want in life because they're unconsciously reacting to everything instead of taking the time to respond. They're making a huge deal out of things that actually aren't that big of a deal and it's ruining the results they're getting! They're investing too much time and mental and emotional energy into things they should brush off, completely ignore, or attend to later. It completely distracts them and robs them of their ability to focus on what's important. In other words, they're too emotionally weak to ignore what doesn't matter. Every little event gets turned into some sort of drama. Traffic sucks - it puts them in a bad mood. They come home and act like a tyrant to the wife and kids because some people they don't know anything about were driving too slowly or got into an accident. They don't control the traffic but they're upset about it. Sounds pretty dumb, huh? Maybe it's something you do. Boss is having a bad day and acts like a dick - they take it personally, make it about themselves, and complain to everyone about it. They use it to get attention and sympathy from their co-workers. Girl doesn't call or text back - their life falls apart and gets put on hold. The workout doesn't get done, they call into work, chores pile up from being neglected, and they lose their focus, drive, and motivation. Everything comes to a screeching halt and falls apart because one girl they barely know isn't giving them attention and approval.

What I've learned from experience is that letting my emotions control my thoughts, decisions, and actions, regardless of the situation, has NEVER been worth it. Every single time I made a big deal out of something, I learned everything would've worked out better had I just relaxed and been cool about it. Easier said than done, I know, but it's possible with effort and willpower. It's possible to stop making a big deal of everything.

The guys embarrassing themselves with women, that might include you, are making a big deal of EVERYTHING their dating life and, more than likely, all other areas of their life. They're creating monster events from tiny things. They're turning baby emotions into colossal emotions. They're turning insignificant little occurrences into life-changing events and seeing them as "signs" that things will or will not work out. Knock that off, dude. Routine and consistency are good for your life and good for your mind. It's extremely important to be consistent in the way you respond to ANY event regardless of how major it is. Before responding, collect as much information as possible. Keep yourself and everyone around you calm. Reacting without information just tells everyone how ignorant and impulsive you are. Not good for your reputation. Collect information, think about how to handle it, move forward intelligently.

The men getting excellent results with women aren't turning anything into a huge deal. Grandma dies - they don't go into hiding, post on social media for sympathy, or cry to women to get attention. They see it as, "Well, yes, she was old. Dying is a part of life. Yes, I love her very much but I accept that this is way the world works and I'm not going to be a baby about it." The girl they like doesn't respond - they don't overreact. They remain calm. They see it as, "Well, shit happens. It is what it is. Instead of freaking out and bugging her, I'll wait and see what happens."

When stressed, YOU ARE MORE ATTRACTIVE WHEN YOU STAY CALM AND RELAXED instead of flipping out and losing your cool like a child. Repeat to yourself every single day, "NOTHING is as big of a deal and most people make it. NOTHING bothers me. NOTHING gets under my skin. NOTHING can make me lose my cool. I can remain calm no matter what."

# #5: I DON'T TAKE IT PERSONALLY WHEN SHE'S UPSET

In my book, **How to Quit Being a Loser with Women**, I talk about how it's OK if women get upset at you because at least while she's upset, you're the center of her attention and she's "feeling" emotions and associating them with you. It's a sign you're not boring or a complete waste of her time. I also talk about how women "stick" to the men who, in one way or another, upset them the most. Not upsetting her like beating and abusing her and cheating on her, but upsetting her by not fitting perfectly into her mold. Not letting her have her way or giving her what she wants 24/7. Not bending to her will and allowing her to toy with you the way most guys do. When she pokes or pushes and you don't react, chances are it may upset her. Look, I know it doesn't make sense and you're like, "WTF is this dude talking about right now, broooo...", but this is VERY, VERY IMPORTANT to understand. If you think long and hard enough about your past experiences with women, and maybe even the experience you're having right now with someone, then you'll begin to understand it better.

Women get upset for SO many reasons and most of them are not ashamed of it. They're just being all emotional and being the way their brain is telling them to be. They're going to push your buttons and test your boundaries. They're going to see what you're made of, how strong you are, and what you can handle. If you have kids, then, you know it's the same thing they unconsciously do. Do you remember thinking, "I'm going to piss my parents off today to see where they'll draw the line with me."? Of course, not! Women aren't consciously or logically doing it! It just happens! Women can be bratty, spoiled, and testy. They can enjoy pushing your buttons and watching you squirm. It doesn't make them bad, mean, or coldhearted. It just makes them... women.

Here's the simple truth, 99% of the women you'll meet, regardless of how much they like you, are going to get upset and bitchy at you at one point or another AND YOU'RE NOT EVEN GOING TO UNDERSTAND WHY THEY'RE UPSET! That's OK. No big deal. There's no way around it. You can't dump every woman in your life because she gets frustrated or upset. The problem isn't women getting upset, that's inevitable. The problem lies in the way most of us handle her being upset or bitchy. When she gets upset and starts shutting down or losing it, that's your golden opportunity to either build more attraction or kill it. It's your opportunity to have more power to control the course of the relationship or give it back so she can use it to reject you. It's your opportunity to make her feel comfortable and safe or misunderstood and involved with the wrong guy.

THE VERY BEST WAY TO HANDLE WHEN WOMEN GET UPSET IS NOT TO REACT TO IT. Yup, that's right. Just don't do anything. Remain calm. Don't say anything. Don't explain yourself. Just chill and listen. This doesn't work well with only women, but with EVERYONE in your life! When you're upset because she's upset, YOU HAVE A PROBLEM and you're making the problem worse. You're fighting fire with fire. You're fighting blind ignorance and anger with blind ignorance and anger. Pretty obvious to see why getting frustrated and upset in return is a terrible idea.

From being on the receiving end of, possibly, hundreds of women being upset at me, I've noticed there's a cycle that happens when she's upset and how you handle the cycle makes or breaks the friendship, relationship, and marriage. The cycle begins when she has a problem with something you said, did, or didn't say or do and she reacts to it. It doesn't matter if it makes sense to you or not. She's not going to take the time to make sure you understand what's happening, I assure you that. Something you did or didn't do hits an emotional nerve and her urge to react takes over. She takes a deep breath and lets you have it. She expresses how she feels, why she feels that way, and how what you're doing or not doing makes her feel. Once she gets it all out and says what she has to say, she begins coming down and feeling relief. Last, once she feels better, she begins reflecting on what just happened AND HOW YOU HANDLED IT!

I'm positive about what I'm saying because, coincidentally, it just happened to me 10 minutes ago! I was sharing something I did with my girlfriend that I thought she would agree with and instead, she took a deep breath and became very frustrated and disagreed with me. You know how I handled it? I remained calm. I didn't raise my voice. I didn't get defensive. I didn't tell her she was wrong. I didn't tell her she was acting like a child. I listened, agreed, told her I understand how she feels and why, and slowly made my exit so she could shower. Whether women have clothes on or not doesn't matter to them. The cycle will happen at any given moment. Be ready to handle it at all times. About a minute ago, she came in, apologized, explained herself, and she's completely calm now. Turns out she had a bad day at work because she works with people who don't think things through and aren't very bright. Not an excuse to rail on me but, again, she's a woman. She's more emotional. Even though she's extremely smart and aware, the cycle still happens. Had I handled it inappropriately, I wouldn't be writing this book at this very moment. We'd be screaming and fighting and calling eachother names like morons and one of us would be storming out. Luckily for me, that's not how things happen in our relationship because I'm able to think clearly and diffuse the situation before it escalates into reality television drama. It makes THAT BIG OF A DIFFERENCE.

Getting upset, trying to prove you're right, or telling her she's dumb while she's in the middle of her cycle is our first instinctive reaction but it's not the smartest one. It's throwing napalm onto an already exploding bomb! If you get upset while she's upset, it leads to a very bad situation and you look like a dumbass who can't keep his head on straight. Remember, she's the more emotional one. This is normal for her! But, for you, as the man, you're supposed to be strong, composed, and a good listener - even if you don't want to! You're supposed to be smart enough to understand it's not a personal attack on you and she's just venting how she feels. You should be smart enough to know that if she didn't give a shit about you, she wouldn't be sharing how she feels with you in that moment. She would literally tell you you're a waste of her time!

So, the better and more attractive way to handle her being upset, obviously, is to remain neutral and calm. Be smart about it. Just listen. It makes her feel safer to express herself and be herself with you. Her cycle ends faster, she feels dumb for getting upset, she's more likely to apologize, and she's less likely to do it in the future because it obviously doesn't affect you or get a rise out of you. Want to add the little cherry on top? Something 99.9% of men DON'T KNOW and DON'T DO? Tell her you agree. That's right. Even if you don't! I'm not asking you to lie. I'm asking you to employ a proven strategy to disarm people, build trust, and keep them from getting, even more, upset with you. Agreeing with people calms them down and opens their mind up to what you have to say. Hey, hostage negotiators do it. Interrogators do it. Psychologists who want you to open up to them do it. It's pure magic! I learned this from one of the top sales experts in the world, Grant Cardone. His number one rule of selling is ALWAYS AGREE WITH THE CUSTOMER. It works miracles.

In the long-term, it is 100X more attractive to be the guy who's calm when she's upset rather than being the guy who takes it personally because he's not smart enough to know the difference.

Before I met my girlfriend, I was seeing a girl who I specifically told I wasn't looking for a relationship or to fall in love. That I wasn't in any position to be getting tied down or married. I made it clear that I understand if it's not what she's looking for. As things progressed, she started showing signs that she was developing feelings. She even told me she wanted to tell me something but then she changed her mind and said she would only say it if I said it first and the fact that I hadn't said it first means she shouldn't say anything. WHAT IN THE WHAT!? Whatever that means. I still don't know. Anyways, one night, on the phone, she wanted to know what she meant to me. I asked her to clarify. She asked where do I see our relationship going. I repeated back to her what I said when I met her - I'm extremely busy, I have a lot of goals to reach, I'm extremely focused, and I don't want to get tied down by anything that will distract me from reaching my goals and hitting my targets. She hung up. Click. What do you think I did? Called her back in a panic and explain myself? Send an army of texts? Send flowers? I was in the bathtub taking an Epsom salt bath because I was sore from working out and I simply set the phone down and enjoyed the rest of my evening as if nothing happened. The next afternoon, I texted her to ask her how her day was and it was as if NOTHING ever happened! A few days later when I was hanging out with her at her apartment, she told me she thought I was never going to talk to her again because she was rude and hung up on me. I told her it wasn't a big deal. She said, and I quote, "I thought it was pretty cute how you texted me all happy the next day like nothing happened."

This is real. The people who react to everything in life wind up on the bottom of the list and in last place. Those who don't take it personally and don't let it bother them win the race and end up on the top of EVERYONE'S list. This is your opportunity to gain serious ground in your life simply by learning how to stop reacting and just handle women being upset at you in a calm, collected, and intelligent way.

# #6 I DON'T TAKE IT PERSONALLY WHEN WOMEN DON'T LIKE ME

One of the first things I learned, and also something else I talk about in **How to Quit Being a Loser with Women** is NOT EVERYONE IS GOING TO LIKE YOU WHEN THEY MEET YOU. Not because you're not a nice person or you don't dress the right way or make the right amount of money, but because we are all different. We all come from different backgrounds, have different upbringings, and our minds are programmed by different people and environments. If you are more aware of this when meeting and interacting with new people, then how much they like you isn't going to matter as much. As you learned earlier in this book, NO ONE thinks and behaves 100% the way you do. Maybe close to it, but not exactly. Taking it personally when someone doesn't like you is a sign that you're ignorant. I didn't say you're stupid or dumb, but ignorant. Ignorant to the fact that we're all different and you can't and don't control other people's thoughts, feelings, and opinions. Yes, you can persuade people to eventually like you more through your behavior and conduct but right now we're focusing on people who don't like you when they're getting to know you.

If you struggle with accepting that not all people are going to like you and worship you, then you are going to consistently struggle with women and fight a lot of unnecessary battles in your mind. You are going to waste A TON of your own time and energy over nothing. Even if you're built like a Greek god and look like a male model from the magazines, a lot of women will still not like you and think you're not they're type. Even if you're the funniest and most likable guy, still, some women will not like you. They'll think you're a clown, you joke around too much, and you're too square for them. When you're too ignorant and inexperienced interacting with women to see what's really going on and you take them not liking you as some kind of personal attack, you create a difficult to overcome mental block that affects the way you interact with women and the way they perceive you. You become so overly obsessed with what they think that you block your ability to relax, think clearly, put on the charm, have fun, and make them laugh. Instead, you think too much, work too hard to get their approval, and kill the attraction.

The reason you have a problem with the idea of people not liking you is because YOU WANT people to like you. You're actively investing time and energy into the idea of people, WHO DON'T KNOW YOU AND DON'T CARE ABOUT YOU as much as you think they do, liking you. Even though it's perfectly natural to want people to like you, the more time and energy you put into getting people to like you and think you're a great guy, the more you drive those same people away and force them to not like you. The biggest secret I've ever learned about getting people to like you and that not enough people know or talk about is that people like you the best when you're not trying to MAKE them like you. The guy who isn't an asshole, doesn't bother anyone, and, at the same time, doesn't care what anyone thinks is usually well-liked guy. People rarely have anything bad to say about him, they want to hang out with him, and they include him in on what's going on. That's the guy you need to be when around women. Chillaxed, not too nosy, and not caring too much what they think and how much they like you.

The guys who attract the most women are the ones who are content with the way women feel about them. They don't fight it or try to change it. They don't take it personally or make it about who they are as a person. They understand everyone is different and everyone is entitled to their own opinion. This is a VERY, VERY powerful mindset that pulls women into your life like a magnet and makes them want to stay there.

# #7 I DON'T WASTE TIME ON PEOPLE WHO DON'T RESPECT ME OR ADD VALUE TO MY LIFE

Also, in my book **Declare War on Yourself - How to Get Your Act and Life Together to Become the Best Version of Yourself**, I talk about how a big part of getting your act together and attracting better women into your life is avoiding those who don't respect you, your time, your wishes, and who don't add value to your life. These people suck the life out of you and make you think less of yourself. They make you feel smaller than you should feel and the worst part of it is that THEY DON'T CARE! They're so focused on themselves and getting meaningless attention that they don't take the time to think about how inconsiderate they're being and how they're making others feel. Your life is too short to surround yourself with ignorant and self-centered people. Draw the line for what you want and only spend time with those who care.

Every second you spend on anyone who doesn't take you seriously costs YOU, not them. You're paying the price for allowing it to happen. Do you say "yes" every single time someone asks you for money or to buy something? I hope not. Why? Because when you give someone YOUR money, YOU PAY THE PRICE, not them. They gain, you lose. When other people are taking value and peace of mind from you by wasting your time, you're paying the price. When I started looking at it this way, everything changed and I became meticulous about how I spent my time. I cut ties with A LOT of people and my life became better. I became happier. As Grant Cardone says, there are 7 billion people on this planet! Quit thinking little. Quit being small-minded. You can afford to dump the people that aren't good for you and surround yourself with the ones who actually are. Quit paying the price for others.

If you're thinking you'll run out of women because you don't waste your time on the ones who don't have their head on straight, then that, right there, is why you're having problems attracting them and keeping them around. You have to quit thinking with such a limited mindset! There are more than enough women to go around. Let go of the ones not adding value to your life and making you happy and replace them with the ones who actually give a damn about themselves and other people.

What I've learned from experience is when you shift your mindset to no longer wasting time on anyone who isn't worthy of it, the women who actually care about you and being in your life will show up and work harder to stay in it. At the same time, when you make that important shift, the women who aren't worth your time will vanish because they can no longer use you. When you drive a certain car, all of a sudden you notice that car everywhere, right? It works the same way when it comes to your mindset. When you think and operate a certain way and you're clear about what you want, you will automatically attract like-minded women. Women who avoid men that waste their time will instantly recognize what you're about and be drawn to you like a magnet. Your friendships and relationships with them will be 10X better, they'll last 10X longer, and they'll make you 10X happier. Instead of wasting your time, they'll support you, be on YOUR side, and make you better.

Here's the kicker - you can't be a piece of shit person and expect everyone to be wonderful to you. Whatever and whomever you want in your life, you have to become the mirror image of it. You are the woman on your arm. If you want higher-quality women who add value to your life and don't waste your time, you have to become a high-quality man who adds value to his own life and doesn't waste his own time.

# #8 I LIKE TO BE IN CONTROL

I've been called a control freak only by women who are out-of-control of themselves and their lives. Interesting. Women who don't like anything in their life to be controlled AT ALL. Women who want to conduct themselves however they want and don't want to face consequences. Women who don't like order and routine. Women who live in constant chaos and drama. Women who can't keep jobs, friendships, or relationships. Higher-quality women who ARE in control of themselves usually don't have a problem with me wanting to assume control of our relationship. They quickly see that my head is in the right place and my desire for control is only for the benefit of everyone involved. They get it.

Being in control means I like to control what's happening to me and around me because I trust myself more than anyone else. I trust MYSELF to get me home safely. I trust MYSELF to make good decisions. I trust MYSELF to get the job done correctly and on time. I trust MYSELF to keep everything in my life running smoothly. I want to control my life. I want to control my environment. I want to control the condition of my home - how clean it is and how organized it is. I want to control the condition of my vehicle - how clean it is and how well it's maintained. I want to control what happens in my life and how much success I can create for myself and that means controlling what I do with my time and how much of it I allow people to take from me. I want to control what happens in my mind and how happy I am. I want to live in MY reality and bring women into it, not the other way around. If I get off on living in another person's reality, it's because I'm not doing enough for myself and to make my life appealing enough. Been there and done that and it's never pushed me in a positive direction. I'd rather people come into and live in my world instead of me living in theirs. I trust MYSELF that the world I'm creating for myself is healthier, higher-quality, and better than the world 99% of other people are creating for themselves.

THIS IS NOT AN EGO THING. I don't want to control other people and their lives. I want to control everything about myself and my life and if anyone insists on being part of my life because of the value they gain from it, or whatever their intention is, I want to control how they treat me and how they conduct themselves while they're in my life. This isn't about controlling women, how they dress, and where they go. This isn't about controlling women's loyalty to you. Women should be allowed to make their own decisions and deal with the consequences of it. THIS IS ABOUT CONTROLLING YOURSELF AND YOUR LIFE. It's important to be extremely clear with yourself on this because control is something MANY men get wrong and abuse. They turn it into something terrible and ruin people's lives with it. Don't take this the wrong way and label me or anyone like me as someone who has a problem. The guy who doesn't care about being in control of himself and what happens in his life is the one with the problem. He's got a BIG PROBLEM and it's messing up every area of his life. Especially his dating life. This guy doesn't attract women.

In order to get the results you actually want with women and for your life to go the way you want it to, you have to take control of everything happening within and around you and not concern yourself with what others say about it. The only people complaining are the ones who don't understand it because they're not in control of themselves or anything in their life. They don't control their mind, emotions, decisions, behavior, and results. They're don't control what happens to them. Ignore them.

Women feel more attraction and respect for the guy who's in control of everything within and around him. They're more attracted to the man who gives a shit about the details of his life and takes consistent action to make sure everything falls into place the way he wants it to.

# #9 THE WORLD IS ABUNDANT

If you honestly believe that there are only so many single women to date and only so many opportunities to meet that perfect woman, you are limiting your own mind and your potential to that reality. The truth is that whatever you believe about the world being limited isn't true. You're just filling your brain with a bunch of garbage that you learned from other limited people and sources and it's sabotaging your success in all areas of your life. The reason you don't take the "abundance" theory seriously is because too many unsuccessful wannabe motivational gurus have made it into a cheesy and corny concept. They don't simplify it enough for most people to understand and believe it. Let me try to help you out with that.

There are more women than you think that are happy to date a guy like you and they're single or about to be single. The problem is that YOU THINK YOU KNOW what type of guy they actually want and who they're looking for without even doing your homework! You're comparing the real world to some movie you saw or what you read in a women's magazine about dating. So, maybe you live in a tiny town where everyone knows everyone and the women you can date is very limited. I've coached plenty of guys with that problem and I always ask "Who's stopping you from moving?" No one. You're limiting YOURSELF to a tiny pond. You're creating your own scarcity. Who said you can't meet women online? No one. You're convinced you only have so many options without even knowing for sure! The more you challenge your mind, beliefs, and reality and do things you haven't done, the more the world will change for you. The more abundant it will become and the more opportunities you'll have. You will prove to YOURSELF that there is more on this planet than you can handle. The type of woman you want - there are so many that you couldn't date them all in 5 lifetimes.

The reason 99% of the money in the world is in 1% of population's hands is because only 1% of the population actually believes they can make and have as much money as they want. The other 99% is stuck in the scarcity mindset of believing they're doomed to certain class of people who can only make a limited amount of money. They're stuck inside the box with a bunch of complainers who are failing to think outside the box.

I used to believe the only way to make money was to get a job working for people who I didn't like and that would be my situation for the rest of my life. That, in order to become rich, I had to have been born into wealth or win the lottery. I was ignorant. My dad programmed me to believe that working as an employee for people I didn't want to be around was the only way to make money. He didn't know any better because he was programmed to believe the same thing by his parents! And that concept WAS true for me until I decided to write books and sell them online. Even when my buddy presented me with the idea, I refused to do it because I believed it wouldn't work! I was stuck in my limited mindset! BUT, the first $19 that I made from selling my Microsoft Word document to a complete stranger in another state changed everything. Since then, I've made more money writing and selling books than having the normal job my dad told me I'd be stuck with! Changing my reality hasn't been any harder than a normal job and it hasn't taken more time. In a normal job, there are things you have to figure out to become good at it. When you learn how stop limiting yourself, change your mindset, get outside of the box that everyone else is in, and accumulate more than you've ever had, you will still have to figure things out! It only involves figuring it out one step at a time. The problem with scarcity-minded people is they don't ever start. Or they do but watching TV and playing on their phone is easier so they do that for the rest of their life. What I'm saying is, YOU have access to ALL of the abundance as much as the men who are "luckier" than you and all you have to do is change your mindset and take action to get it. 99% OF PEOPLE WON'T DO IT and it gives you THAT BIG of an advantage! If I didn't go through the process, you wouldn't be reading this book right now and improving your dating life, would you? I wouldn't be able to help you. All I did was Google how to write eBooks and figured out the rest from there. I Googled thousands of different topics so I could learn how to make this book possible! I invested time and energy into changing my reality and the rest of my life. What's stopping you from doing the same? Who's stopping you from changing your mindset? Only YOU.

The abundance mindset is understanding there is more than you can possibly imagine and you and your mindset are in your way. The only other roadblocks you face are the people you surround yourself with who tell you "all the good women are taken. Women like that don't want guys like us. We aren't tall enough for them. We don't make enough money. They only like snobby jerks." Complete and utter bullshit, bro. None of that is true. It's only true TO YOU because you believe it.

Look, I'm only 5 feet 6 inches tall. I'm short. "Women don't like short guys", right? Wrong. I've dated beautiful women who are 5'10, 5'11, and so on who were crazy about me. Hey, we're all the same height laying down. If you gotta put your toes on her knees and push up to get a little deeper in there, then do what you gotta do, bud! I'm talking about women so tall that I had to go "up" on them, know what I mean? If they wanted to be in serious relationships within a week of meeting me, then my height wasn't an issue, was it? They never once said "I didn't measure up" or "I was coming up short". I attracted them with what you're learning in this book right now and they didn't mind me climbing up those long legs every night and doing push-ups on 'em.

Women don't want limited-minded guys who can only provide them with limited experiences and a limited life. They don't want men whose mind is stuck in the mode of believing the world is scarce and limited. When you believe ANYTHING is possible, you will attract and date women you never thought would date you or want to be in your life. You will find yourself in situations that feel like you're in a movie. You will look back at how limited your life was before and be completely amazed at how far you've come and how much has changed. It only takes making that shift in your mindset from "the world is limited and only lucky people get the things I want" to "the world is abundant and anything I want at anytime, it's available for anyone to have".

The abundance factor only activates in your life when you believe it exists and you take action to get everything you've ever wanted. When you take action to make the things you want to happen, happen. If you don't take action, nothing will ever happen and the other "lucky" guys that you love to envy will continue getting luckier and luckier because they're doing what you refuse to do. When I was 25 years old, my roommate used to make fun me because, while he was out drinking, partying, chasing women, and losing his money to other people in poker, I stayed in my bedroom in front of a computer screen filling my mind with as much information as possible on women, dating, business, and life. He'd invite me out and make sarcastic comments when I told him I couldn't go because I have a lot of information to cover and it needs to get done ASAP. Fast-forward 10 years - we're 35-years-old now. He STILL goes and plays poker, chases women, and drinks, not so much partying, BUT he currently lives with his mom and dad and stays in the same room he grew up in. I'm not talking trash, we still associate, but I worked to change my mind and behavior A LOT more than he did and now our lives are night and day. I LIVE IN ABUNDANCE and have more than I need while he struggles to make ends meet and provide for him and his son. The only difference between me and him is I CHOSE TO TAKE CONSTANT ACTION while he chose to do the opposite. There's a lot to be learned from that.

# #10 NO TIME FOR NEGATIVITY

The effect being positive has on women is profound and it makes them feel better about themselves when they're with you, around you, and away from you. Look, most of the guys they meet are negative and what have I taught you in this book? Be different. Most guys that women meet aren't focused on the positive. They're average and thinking average thoughts. Your happiness comes first and part of protecting your happiness and peace of mind is blocking out negativity at all costs.

On the old radios that you have to turn the knob to find a station, my brother Will says that negativity is like that static in between the stations. It provides no value and everyone skips right past it. Just like that old radio, we should skip past all negativity until we find something worth listening to. If you wouldn't sit around and listen to the static on that old radio, why are you listening to negativity and garbage in your life? Why are you spreading it? It's a complete waste of your time.

The more negativity you allow, the more you're poisoning your own mind. The more negativity you allow to come out of your mouth, the more you're brainwashing yourself and those around you. You're blending in with the rest of the herd and thinking like they do. The herd being the people who bitch, complain, and whine and don't get what they want in life. They don't get the women and the dating life they want. The more you blend in with the herd, the more negative people and women you attract into your life. That negativity just multiplies and multiplies and your life gets worse and worse and you feel worse and worse. To turn it around, you have to break the pattern. Break the cycle. Pull the negativity needle out. Quit being hooked on it.

When someone is being negative, I cut them off as soon as I can and tell them, "Hey, I don't care to talk about this and I don't have time for it.

Listening to it doesn't benefit me and me letting you go on about it won't benefit you, either." If I have to sound like a jerk and they get upset, I'm OK with that. Someone being mad at me is better than letting someone infiltrate my mindset and poison it with garbage. I also ask women, "Is there a particular reason you're being so negative? There are so many positive aspects to what you're talking about and all I'm hearing is why you don't like it. You would do yourself a huge favor if you chose to focus on what's good about it. The situation would probably improve." I don't care who it is. If they're being negative, I'm going to walk away or stop them in their tracks and let them know it's not allowed around me, in my home, or anywhere that's important to me. YOU ARE IN CONTROL of the negativity that invades your space. You're definitely in control of the negativity that comes out of your face. Wipe it out of your mind, get away from negative people, get rid of the negative stuff on your phone, and stop watching it on TV. Definitely stop sharing it on social media. It makes you look like a crybaby and a pussy. Just being honest.

Small, weak, and defeated minds focus on the bad. The things that hurt. The things that are uncomfortable. The things that upset them. Strong minds block it all out and only focus on that little bit of light instead of all of the darkness. It's easier for weaker and smaller minds to feel victimized, attacked, and defeated. To feel alone and like no one cares. They coddle themselves and want people to feel sorry for them. When you're mentally and emotionally tougher, that nonsense doesn't even cross your mind! You're embarrassed to be any kind of victim! It's pathetic to you. If you're being attacked, you strike back fast and hard to end it. You never feel defeated because only quitters and wimps give up. You never feel alone and discarded because you have yourself and you give more of a shit about your own life than anyone around you so, "alone" isn't in your vocabulary. Being positive isn't about being cheesy and corny, it's about being mentally tough and controlling your mind.

# CONCLUSION: MEN WHO WANT TO CONTINUOUSLY IMPROVE ATTRACT MORE WOMEN

The average American reads 1 - 4 books per year and the average CEO reads 5 books per month. The facts don't lie and the numbers in their bank accounts definitely don't lie. The person always striving to improve does WAY better than the person who doesn't really care about improving. That includes women and dating. The typical guy who's slaying it with women, that means doing good, and he isn't rich or unusually good-looking is in one way or another working on himself on a regular basis. Either he's learning how to communicate with people better, he's learning about women and dating by reading books like this, or he's doing everything he can to take care of and improve his body and mind on a daily basis. He's continuously improving. The men at the very top are doing ALL OF IT, which is a lot of work, but worth it.

Billionaires read more books than the average CEO. Bill Gates, one of the richest men in the world said if he could have a superpower, it would be to read faster. Warren Buffett, another one of the world's richest men, read 8 HOURS PER DAY! They're at the top, but they STILL put a lot of time, effort, and energy into improving who they are. What's your excuse? Why are you investing all of your time into playing Fortnite when you could be learning things that will benefit you for the rest of your life?

Fill your mind with information. There's so much to know about this world and I guarantee you the more you learn about it, the more you will find a way to incorporate it into your ability to attract women. It's no surprise or coincidence that women complain with such disgust about their ex-boyfriends and ex-husbands who refused to improve and do better for themselves. It's no surprise they're no longer with them! I've seen it time and time again and I have never seen a man who has no interest in improving his mindset, behavior, and life attract, date, and keep high-quality women around. It just doesn't happen. They only attract small-minded, problematic, and low-quality women and the relationships they have with them are full of lies, deceit, manipulation, and problems. They're getting out of life what they're putting into it, which is nothing!

If you want more out of your dating life and out of life, in general, you have to start putting more into it. The more you invest into yourself, the more you're going to see it manifest in all areas of your life. I'm not trying to sound all woo-woo and spiritual but it is absolutely true. Something positive will always happen in your life when you cram your brain full of positive information and only negative things will happen when you cram your brain full of negative information. It's that simple.

If you want more women in your life and women who are more mature, caring, respectful, and less-problematic, you have to take action to make that happen. You have to improve yourself and develop a more attractive mindset. Look, the reason I didn't talk about how to dress, groom, and speak in this book is because I'm not that shallow and ignorant. That stuff REALLY doesn't matter if you have an advanced mindset. I know too well that clothes and words don't make the big difference you're looking for. They're only a short-lived crutch that too many men depend on and wonder why they aren't seeing big changes. Mindset trumps EVERYTHING! Improving your mindset will create the fastest and most radical changes in your life and attract the women you've been wanting to attract. The more you improve your mindset and everything about yourself, the more women you're going to attract and with less effort.

# 2nd Edition

# HOW ATTRACTING WOMEN REALLY WORKS

## by Marc Summers

Thank you for reading this book and I hope I was able to expand your mind, help you out, and solve a lot of problems for you. Keep in mind that books like this are more helpful and effective when you read them or listen to them at least 2 to 3 times because each time, you're going to see or hear something you didn't before. I invest hundreds of hours into putting each one of these books together and if I missed anything or there's something you believe I can improve, do not hesitate to email me at **marc@majorleaguedating.com** and let me know. Once again, thank you very much for taking the time to read my book and if I didn't have your continued support, I wouldn't be able to continually push myself to create new content and find new ways to help you as much as possible. It's with great humility that I thank you from the bottom of my heart and wish you the very best of luck in accomplishing your goals. I am forever grateful for you. Please take a minute to **go to majorleaguedating.com and check out my other products** that'll help you out just as much as this one did.

# PLEASE REVIEW THIS BOOK:

Hey, it's Marc. Thank you very much for reading this book. If it helped you understand women, dating, and attraction better and believe it'll help you solve a lot of problems, **please go to amazon.com and leave me a 5 star review and positive feedback for this book**. It only takes 10 seconds and helps me more than you know. Thank you again.

*- Marc Summers*

## Customer Reviews

☆☆☆☆☆ 71
4.9 out of 5 stars ▾

| | | |
|---|---|---|
| 5 star | | 92% |
| 4 star | | 7% |
| 3 star | | 1% |
| 2 star | | 0% |
| 1 star | | 0% |

Share your thoughts

Write a customer review

See all 71 customer reviews ›

# WORKBOOK: HOW ATTRACTING WOMEN REALLY WORKS

# Workbook

# HOW ATTRACTING WOMEN REALLY WORKS

by Marc Summers

# HOW TO USE THIS WORKBOOK

This workbook is specifically designed to make you go through the book with a fine-toothed comb and THINK. The more I make you think, take a second look at what I said, and use your brain, the better you're going to remember what's in this book. According to research, we only retain 10% of what we read and you'll retain 5X that amount if you have to go back and find specific and important points.

Not only do I want you to go through the book and find the information that goes with the question, but I also want you to add to the answer using your own thoughts and judgement. I don't want you to just copy word for word what the answer is so you can move on and be done with it. That's what kids do and you're not just doing this for a simple grade. THIS IS FOR YOUR LIFE AND HAPPINESS! I want you to do this for yourself so you can improve how women respond to you and improve the quality of your dating life. I'm asking you not to be lazy here. The effort you put into this is what you're going to get out of it.

I want you to cram this information so far down into your brain that you forget it's there BUT you're still able to remember it in front of women and use it to think clearly about what you're doing or about to do. If you're in a situation and the information isn't there, you're screwed! Right? But, if it is there because you actually DID THE WORK to put it there, then, even if you need it only once over the next 5 years, you'll be glad you had access to it in that moment.

Knowledge alone isn't power. You should know that already. Power is KNOWING WHAT TO DO WITH KNOWLEDGE WHEN YOU NEED IT. It's knowing how to apply the knowledge in situations requiring it. Action without knowledge is useless as well but action WITH knowledge makes you incredibly powerful in the moment.

THE BEST DATING TIPS, HELP, & SOLUTIONS – MAJORLEAGUEDATING.COM

# PART 1: 10
# ATTRACTION
# DESTROYING
# MINDSETS

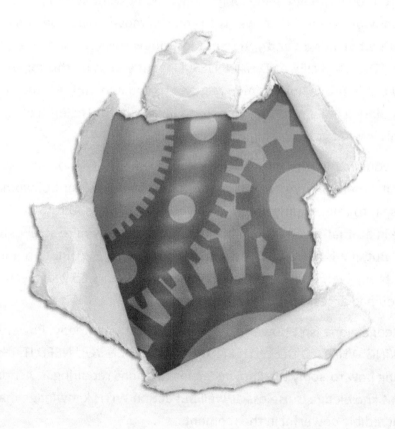

Why is it extremely important to learn which mindsets kill attraction?

_____

_____

_____

_____

_____

What do I mean by having your mind put together?

_____

_____

_____

_____

_____

What is the most important tool you have to attract women and why?

_____

_____

_____

_____

_____

# #1: THINKING YOU HAVE TO BE NICE NO MATTER WHAT

Why is being nice to women in order to get them to give you something in return ineffective?

_____

_____

_____

_____

_____

What is the thing most men don't understand about being nice to women and why is it important?

_____

_____

_____

_____

_____

How does being overly nice to women make you look and, if they're honest enough, what will most women tell you about how they feel about it?

_____

_____

_____

_____

_____

Why is being overly nice a weak mindset?

_____

_____

_____

_____

_____

What happens to your inauthentic niceness towards women when you value yourself, have a sense of self-worth, handle your own emotional needs, and don't care about getting validation from anyone?

_____

_____

_____

_____

_____

What is a big reason women are attracted to jerks?

_____

_____

_____

_____

_____

Instead of being overly nice or being a complete jerk to women, what mindset seems to work best?

_____

_____

_____

_____

_____


What are you afraid of doing when you're overly nice to women and how does it negatively impact your chances or relationship with her? What more effective things can you do instead that build 10X more attraction?

_____

_____

_____

_____

_____

_____

_____

_____

_____

_____

If, after all of these years of crashing and burning, you're still using "nice" as your main strategy, what could be the reason behind it?

_____

_____

_____

_____

_____

Why won't most women come straight out and tell you you're being too nice and tell you how it actually makes them feel?

_____

_____

_____

_____

_____

Instead of looking at women like they're above you and you're below them, how should you view them?

_____

_____

_____

_____

_____

# #2: THINKING YOU NEED TO IMPRESS HER

Why is impressing women completely different from making them feel actual attraction?

_____

_____

_____

_____

_____

Which men are women most impressed with?

_____

_____

_____

_____

_____

Instead of impressing women, who should you focus on impressing and why?

_____

_____

_____

_____

_____

What steps can you take towards impressing yourself more?

_____

_____

_____

_____

_____

What are some things you don't like about yourself right now THAT YOU
CAN ACTUALLY CHANGE so you'll be more impressed with yourself?

_____

_____

_____

_____

_____

_____

_____

_____

_____

_____

What steps are you going to take towards changing those things?

_____

_____

_____

_____

_____

_____

_____

_____

_____

_____

What's wrong with seeking approval from other people who don't care about you as much as you think?

_____

_____

_____

_____

_____

What's the difference between approval from other people vs. approval from yourself?

_____

_____

_____

_____

_____

What are you doing right now in your life to impress women and what do you need to do to change so you'll stop doing it?

_____

_____

_____

_____

_____

If you want to attract women and make them feel things they usually don't feel for other men, what do you have to do?

_____

_____

_____

_____

_____

# #3: CARING TOO MUCH IF SHE LIKES YOU OR NOT

If you want women to actually like you and feel attraction for you, what do you have to stop doing?

_____

_____

_____

_____

_____

If you spend too much time and energy consciously thinking about how much she likes you, what is more likely to happen?

_____

_____

_____

_____

_____

What is the most effective mindset to have when it comes to women liking you?

_____

_____

_____

_____

What is important to accept when it comes to women and people liking you?

_____
_____
_____
_____
_____

What is the shortcut to attraction that most guys don't get?

_____
_____
_____
_____
_____

If you don't like who you are, what do you need to do starting today?

_____
_____
_____
_____
_____

# #4 THINKING GIVING HER APPROVAL GETS APPROVAL

What are 4 problems with giving approval to get approval in return?

_____

_____

_____

_____

_____

_____

_____

_____

_____

What are 4 benefits of withholding approval and not giving it away freely?

_____

_____

_____

_____

_____

_____

_____

_____

_____

Why is withholding approval not manipulation or game playing in any way?

_____
_____
_____
_____
_____

Women are more committed to you when they have to what?

_____
_____
_____
_____
_____

# #5: THINKING YOU AREN'T GOOD ENOUGH FOR HER

If you aren't good enough for yourself, then you'll never...

_____

_____

_____

_____

_____

If you ARE good enough for yourself but you still think she's out of your league, what is the right mindset to have?

_____

_____

_____

_____

_____

If you don't feel you're good enough for women, you have the power to at least do what?

_____

_____

_____

_____

_____

# #6: THINKING TELLING HER HOW YOU FEEL WILL DO THE TRICK

What is one thing that screws up a lot of potential relationships?

_____

_____

_____

_____

_____

From the experience I talk about, what happened when women were the first to say how they felt?

_____

_____

_____

_____

_____

In order to quit messing things up with women when I was experiencing emotion and feelings, how did I change my approach?

_____

_____

_____

_____

_____

How did I treat the women I didn't like as much differently from the women liked a lot? What kind of difference did it make?

_____

_____

_____

_____

_____

Now that I'm better able to control myself and not say anything when I'm feeling emotions, what happens NOW that is normal and just something I completely expect to happen?

_____

_____

_____

_____

_____

What rule do I use for friendships and relationships and what EXACTLY does it entail? How will this rule improve your own relationships?

_____

_____

_____

_____

_____

_____

_____

_____

When women reveal anything about how they feel about you, what are you NEVER supposed to do and why?

_____

_____

_____

_____

_____

What is the golden rule to use when you're having "feelings" and emotions? You're supposed to stick to this rule even if it means what?

_____

_____

_____

_____

_____

# #7: THINKING ATTRACTION IS ALL ABOUT LOOKS AND MONEY

What did I point out about my friend's emotional mindset that makes it easier for him to attract women?

_____

_____

_____

_____

_____

What did I point out about the way my friend interacts with people that makes it easier for him to attract women?

_____

_____

_____

_____

_____

How often does he run his mouth and tell people what he's thinking and feeling?

_____

_____

_____

_____

_____

What did I point out about the way my friend moves around that makes it easier for him to attract women?

_____

_____

_____

_____

_____


What is it about my friend's behavior when he's around women that causes him to stand out to them?

_____

_____

_____

_____

_____

# #8: THINKING THE WORD "NO" WILL MAKE HER RUN AWAY

What happens when women see you're mentally weak and submissive and you don't stick up for yourself?

_____

_____

_____

_____

_____

When you can't say no, not only to women, but to everyone else you interact with, what are you inviting into your life?

_____

_____

_____

_____

_____

What does the word "no" help you protect? What happens when women sense your personal boundary and border?

_____

_____

_____

_____

_____

# #9: THINKING SHE'LL FREAK OUT IF YOU GET PHYSICAL

From experience, how do I know if she has NO PROBLEM with me touching her or getting physical with her?

_____

_____

_____

_____

_____

If women are having a great time with you, what is it they probably want and don't mind you doing?

_____

_____

_____

_____

_____

What happens when you initiate contact sooner than later? Why is it important?

_____

_____

_____

_____

_____

What powerful effect does physical touch have on women?

_____

_____

_____

_____

_____

How do you know if it's OK to touch her in any way?

_____

_____

_____

_____

If you're not sure whether or not it's OK to touch her, what should you do?

_____

_____

_____

_____

_____

What can women sense from a mile away?

_____

_____

_____

If you want to create and build tons of attraction, then you cannot be what?

_____

_____

_____

_____

_____

If it's not the right time, too soon, or she, literally, doesn't want you touching her, what is the right thing to do? What is the right mindset to have?

_____

_____

_____

_____

_____

# #10: THINKING SHE THINKS THE WAY YOU DO

What is the biggest thing stopping you from creating, building, and maintaining deep and real attraction with women?

_____

_____

_____

_____

_____

The men who are having the worst "luck" with women and failing in their dating life are doing so because of what?

_____

_____

_____

_____

_____

Before I decided to do whatever it took to turn my dating life around and develop the ability to attract women faster and easier, I failed to realize what?

_____

_____

_____

_____

_____

What is the problem with wanting, wishing, and simple-mindedly believing women SHOULD think, respond, and feel the way you do?

_____

_____

_____

_____

_____

If you ever find yourself struggling and getting upset because women don't think like you, what is the most important thing you can do?

_____

_____

_____

_____

_____

If you're getting bad results with women, you're upset that they're not functioning the way you want them to, and you actually believe THEY'RE the ones with the problem, it means what?

_____

_____

_____

_____

_____

# PART 2: A DEEPER LOOK INTO ATTRACTION

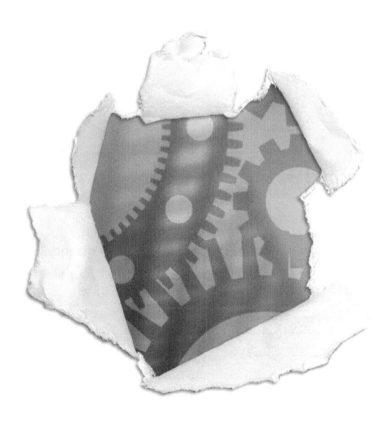

# PERSONAL MAGNETISM

What happens if your mind and life are in constant disagreement, confusion, and misdirection? What do women notice about it?

_____

_____

_____

_____

_____

What happens when your mind and life are both on the same page and focused on the same goals? What do women notice about it?

_____

_____

_____

_____

_____

Just like a "filled" shell of an atom sabotages its own magnetic capabilities, how does a "filled mind" affect you and your ability to attract women?

_____

_____

_____

_____

_____

When your mind resembles the "filled" shell of an atom, it's a collection of what?

_____

_____

_____

_____

_____

Just like a molding and rotten sponge full of old water, a rotten and stale mind doesn't what?

_____

_____

_____

_____

_____

What does a "filled" mind cause you to do in your dating life?

_____

_____

_____

_____

_____

Rather than being the magnetic person that pulls women in, your "filled mind" does what?

_____

_____

_____

_____

_____

When your mind resembles the atom with a "half-filled" shell, it's almost inevitable that what? What's happening in your mind?

_____

_____

_____

_____

_____

_____

_____

_____

_____

_____

Along with refusing to be a know-it-all, you're willing to what?

_____

_____

_____

_____

_____

Once you understand the basic concept of personal magnetism, eliminate the nonsense, and your thoughts, emotions, and behavior all serve a specific purpose, what happens?

_____

_____

_____

_____

_____

What happens when you don't understand the concept of personal magnetism?

_____

_____

_____

_____

_____

Convincing her to like you, buying flowers and dinner, and telling her how much you like her doesn't what?

_____

_____

_____

_____

_____

# WOMEN'S BRAIN STRUCTURE

One consistent finding throughout time is that the hippocampus, part of the limbic system, is what in women's brains?

_____

_____

_____

_____

_____

Researchers and scientists believe the larger hippocampus explains what about women?

_____

_____

_____

_____

_____

Awareness of women's superior ability to feel and process emotion and why they do it is your first step to what?

_____

_____

_____

_____

_____

The difference isn't just in her background, upbringing, education, religion, or perception and understanding of the world. It's also the...

_____

_____

_____

_____

_____

# MEN ARE MORE LOGICAL

The human brain is made of two cerebral hemispheres - the left and the right. The left hemisphere is, theoretically, responsible for what?

_____

_____

_____

_____

_____

The right hemisphere is, theoretically, responsible for what?

_____

_____

_____

_____

_____

In males, greater neural connectivity was found from font to back within each hemisphere suggesting what about men's brains?

_____

_____

_____

_____

_____

This explains why it's easier for men to...

_____

_____

_____

_____

_____

And why men are able to become so...

_____

_____

_____

_____

_____

# WOMEN ARE MORE EMOTIONAL

Since connectivity is greater BETWEEN the left and right hemispheres, it facilitates communication between analytical and intuitive. What does this mean?

_____

_____

_____

_____

_____

Like Mr. Gungor said, when we're in our mental "box", we stay in that box. Women, on the other hand, connect everything to everything and, from The National Academy of Science's neurological map of the female brain, explains why so many women...

_____

_____

_____

_____

_____

The results of the 521 female and 428 male brain scans suggest male brains appear to be better optimized for…

_____

_____

_____

_____

_____

And female brains appear to be better optimized for…

_____

_____

_____

_____

_____

As a man, you're more likely to come to answers and conclusions using

_____.

Women, on the other hand, are more likely to come to answers and conclusions using _____.

When it comes to attracting women, most of us attempt to get women to like us by...

_____

_____

_____

_____

_____

# THE 10% - 15% DIFFERENCE

What have my interactions with women, including short-term and long-term relationships and, even, living with them for years at a time have revealed?

_____

_____

_____

_____

_____

The purpose is to suggest that the 10% - 15% difference between the male and female mind is where...

_____

_____

_____

_____

_____

When women consider you a "stranger" because they don't know you, what exists between you and her?

_____

_____

_____

_____

_____

It's there because of what?

_____

_____

_____

_____

_____

She doesn't know that part of you and making assumptions, on her part, is what?

_____

_____

_____

_____

_____

In order to locate her attraction button and pound it so she feels the emotion and attraction you want her to feel, it's important to...

_____

_____

_____

_____

You can point out the 85% - 90% of commonalities you and her share all day long and, at best, it'll only do what?

_____

_____

_____

_____

_____

Her attraction button is NO WHERE NEAR what?

_____

_____

_____

_____

_____

She can easily find these general commonalities with most men but it doesn't guarantee what?

_____

_____

_____

_____

_____

Never make a big deal about what?

_____

_____

_____

This 10% - 15% difference between the male and female mind is where...

_____

_____

_____

_____

_____

When you meet women, before you open your mouth to sell yourself and say what she's likely heard other men say, what do you need to do?

_____

_____

_____

_____

_____

There are two ways to do this. The first is to what? What will you quickly learn?

_____

_____

_____

_____

_____

_____

_____

_____

_____

When she sees you understand this, what happens?

_____

_____

_____

_____

_____

The second way is to what?

_____

_____

_____

_____

_____

You communicate this through what?

_____

_____

_____

_____

_____

Every little thing you say and do and the way it's said and done conveys what?

_____

_____

_____

_____

_____

The more she likes what she sees and hears, the more...

_____

_____

_____

_____

_____

Both approaches work best when you what?

_____

_____

_____

_____

_____

# PART 3: MAKING THE MENTAL SHIFT

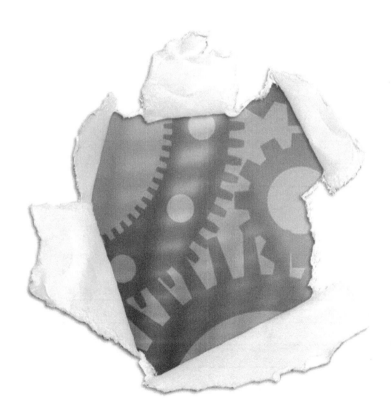

# THE IMPORTANT MENTAL SHIFT

More success with women means doing what?

_____

_____

_____

_____

_____

Designing your thinking, behavior, and responses doesn't mean what?
What does it mean instead?

_____

_____

_____

_____

_____

Making this important mental shift means...

_____

_____

_____

_____

_____

How does your mindset shift?

_____

_____

_____

_____

_____

# LIKING ISN'T ATTRACTION

Men who struggle to attract women make the rookie mistake of doing what?

_____

_____

_____

_____

_____

Her liking you is much different from what?

_____

_____

_____

_____

_____

What state of mind is she in when she "likes" you?

_____

_____

_____

_____

_____

What state of mind is she in when she's feeling attraction?

_____

_____

_____

_____

_____

When she only likes you, she's what?

_____

_____

_____

_____

_____

When she's feeling attraction, she's what?

_____

_____

_____

_____

_____

Instead of getting women to like you, what should you focus on?

_____

_____

_____

_____

_____

Why is convincing her you're a nice and great guy not a good idea and a waste of time?

_____

_____

_____

_____

_____

# WOMEN DON'T THINK ATTRACTION

Women _____ attraction. They don't think it.

What else don't women do when it comes to attraction?

_____
_____
_____
_____
_____

Doing things women don't naturally respond to does what?

_____
_____
_____
_____
_____

What are examples of boring, too logical, and not emotionally stimulating things that women don't respond well to?

_____
_____
_____
_____
_____

Things to "show" her what kind of guy you are don't spark attraction because of what?

_____

_____

_____

_____

_____

# SHE CAN DISLIKE YOU AND STILL FEEL ATTRACTION

Why is it that sometimes you'll meet women who, for some reason or another, won't like you as a person but still want a sexual relationship with you?

_____

_____

_____

_____

_____

If, when she thinks of you, her mind goes to a cold, callus, and purely logical place, what happens to your chances of her feeling attraction?

_____

_____

_____

_____

_____

Why is it extremely common for a scorned woman, from an emotional mindset, to talk passionately about how much she hates or dislikes a certain guy?

_____

_____

_____

_____

_____


Her being pissed at you is far better than what?

_____

_____

_____

_____

_____


At least, when she's pissed, she's associating emotion with you. The "feelings" are triggering her to what?

_____

_____

_____

_____

_____

# TRIGGERING EMOTION MATTERS

When she's feeling attraction, her powerful emotions override what logic?

_____

_____

_____

_____

_____

What happens in her mind when she's logically trying to protect herself?

_____

_____

_____

_____

_____

All of a sudden, she doesn't care if she doesn't know you. Your face, age, height, weight, financial status, and friends aren't as important anymore. The way you're making her "feel" becomes more important than what?

_____

_____

_____

_____

_____

Women gush about the man they want, but what's the truth behind the man they actually choose to be with?

_____

_____

_____

_____

_____

Triggering emotion is the...

_____

_____

_____

_____

_____

# EMOTIONS GUIDE HER ACTIONS

Emotions and feelings override...

_____

_____

_____

_____

_____

When her feelings and emotions take over, how quickly and easily can she go from out of your league to in your league?

_____

_____

_____

_____

_____

What happens when you stir up emotion, access her attraction button, and pound on it?

_____

_____

_____

_____

_____

What are her emotions influencing?

_____
_____
_____
_____
_____

Just like she can't choose whether or not to be attracted to you, she also can't choose what?

_____
_____
_____
_____
_____

She can choose what to do about the emotions she's feeling but she can't what?

_____
_____
_____
_____
_____

When you notice the objective to subjective mindset shift happening, it means what?

_____

_____

_____

_____

_____

# PART 4:
# ATTRACTION
# POWER

# YOU CONTROL HOW SHE FEELS

What happens when she's feeling emotion that's continually transformed into deep and heavy attraction? What does she NOT control?

_____
_____
_____
_____
_____

Who ACTUALLY controls it and why?

_____
_____
_____
_____
_____

When she's feeling a lot of emotion and attraction, what can't her friends, family, her, and even, you, do?

_____
_____
_____
_____
_____

With this power comes great maturity and responsibility. In this highly-emotional state, women are...

_____

_____

_____

_____

_____

And it means you shouldn't do what?

_____

_____

_____

_____

_____

# SHE WILL GIVE YOU HER POWER

When building attraction, it's important to understand what?

_____
_____
_____
_____
_____

Biologically, she needs the power for what?

_____
_____
_____
_____
_____

You, on the other hand, need the power to do what?

_____
_____
_____
_____
_____

When she agrees to hang out or go on a date with you, she kisses you, sleeps with you, agrees to become your girlfriend, and so on, you feel the power do what?

_____

_____

_____

_____

_____

When you feel the power moving in your direction, you're developing what? What does it do?

_____

_____

_____

_____

_____

When she has all of the power and you have very little to none, like when you first meet her, she has what? What does she use it for?

_____

_____

_____

_____

_____

When the power transfers from her to you, its _____ doesn't change. Only its _____ changes.

When she has the power, it's used for _____. When you have it, it's used to _____.

When she feels the transfer of power happening and she's comfortable with it, how close is she paying attention to you? What is she watching for?

_____

_____

_____

_____

_____

What happens if you get weird, clingy, needy, and emotionally weak and confess your love for her?

_____

_____

_____

_____

_____

What happens if you're relaxed and cool about everything and don't make a big deal about it?

_____

_____

_____

_____

_____

No matter how amazing the power feels, always do what?

_____

_____

_____

_____

_____

What don't most men don't know or understand about this power and women's relationship with it and why?

_____

_____

_____

_____

_____

Simply put, what type of man do all women want?

_____

_____

_____

_____

_____

For there to be any transfer of power, she has to what?

_____

_____

_____

_____

_____

If she IS feeling attraction, how soon the transfer of power takes place depends on what?

_____

_____

_____

_____

_____

If you're very experienced with women, you understand their thoughts and emotions, you're very good at communicating, and you know how to hold and conduct yourself in an attractive manner, how long does the transfer of power take to begin?

_____

_____

_____

_____

_____

If you're still learning and haven't experienced a lot of success and failure with women, which is vital to getting better, how long does the process usually take and why?

_____

_____

_____

_____

_____

When she's more experienced with men, why does she have more rejection power? Why is she more protective of it?

_____

_____

_____

_____

_____

The more naïve she is and the less experienced she is with men, if she hands over all of her rejection power within the first day or week, then what is the smart way to handle it?

_____

_____

_____

_____

_____


The attraction power and rejection power work in perfect balance. They're harmonious. The power can move in which directions?

_____

_____

_____

_____

_____

Think about the times you inadvertently gave your attraction power back to her. What was it you did, that you can remember, that caused it to happen and how did it affect the relationship? How fast did it happen? Be honest. The more honest you are, the more you learn and grow.

_____
_____
_____
_____
_____
_____
_____
_____
_____
_____
_____
_____
_____
_____
_____
_____
_____
_____
_____
_____
_____
_____

When you notice your attraction power is leaking out through holes in your mindset, behavior, and habits and she's losing attraction for you through tiny, and seemingly unnoticeable, reactions and behaviors, what is important to do?

_____

_____

_____

_____

_____

From now on, with ANY woman you meet, keep in mind that the more power she senses the has over you, the more likely she is to what?

_____

_____

_____

_____

_____

The power only begins to move when she is what?

_____

_____

_____

_____

_____

# SHE DOESN'T WANT YOU TO GIVE THE POWER BACK

What is something else that will set you apart from other men and that women will thank you for and why?

_____

_____

_____

_____

_____

What are women looking for you to understand and do?

_____

_____

_____

_____

_____

There's nothing more frustrating, conflicting, disappointing, and heartbreaking to women than what?

_____

_____

_____

_____

_____

How does it actually make women feel when you don't turn out to be the man they're hoping you are and that they desperately want you to be?

_____

_____

_____

_____

_____

When the transfer of power happens, what is happening in her mind?

_____

_____

_____

_____

_____

When you're not doing all of the "logical" things other men are doing, she will give you her power and let you keep it. What are some of these logical things?

_____

_____

_____

_____

_____

_____

_____

_____

_____

When it comes to your attraction power, what can she not do?

_____

_____

_____

_____

_____

Don't make the naïve, clueless, and rookie mistake of thinking what?

_____

_____

_____

_____

_____

No matter how bad things get or how desperate you are, what should you NEVER do with your attraction power?

_____

_____

_____

The worst part about giving the power back is what?

_____

_____

_____

_____

_____

# KEEPING THE POWER FOR YOURSELF KEEPS HER FEELING ATTRACTION

To keep your attraction power, which things do you need to stop doing?

_____

_____

_____

_____

_____

_____

_____

_____

_____

_____

When A PERMANENT shift happens in your mind, what happens to your thinking and behavior?

_____

_____

_____

_____

_____

The simplest way of keeping your attraction is power and not giving it back to her is to always what?

_____

_____

_____

_____

_____

# PART 5: POWERFUL MINDSETS THAT SPARK AND KEEP ATTRACTION

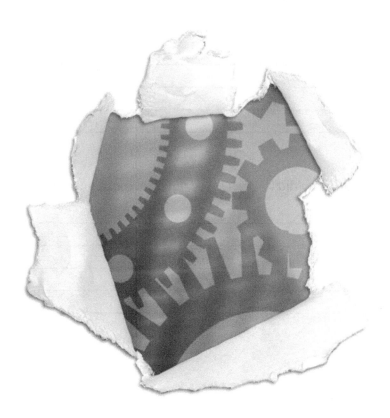

# ALWAYS KEEP IN MIND THAT WOMEN ARE SKEPTICAL

Be completely honest. In what ways have you thought you were smarter than women and others around you so you can get away with something or get something out of it?

_____

_____

_____

_____

_____

_____

_____

_____

_____

In the long run, how did it catch up to you and make you look bad?

_____

_____

_____

_____

_____

What strict standards can you set for your mind and behavior that'll help you get better results with women and everyone around you?

_____

_____

_____

_____

_____

When and where are you not being completely straightforward with yourself, women, and others in your life?

_____

_____

_____

_____

_____

What can you do to begin being more straightforward - even if it doesn't put you in the best position?

_____

_____

_____

_____

_____

You are the most trustworthy when you...

_____

_____

_____

_____

_____

If your answers are too perfect, she assumes what?

_____

_____

_____

_____

_____

If your answers catch her off guard and surprise her, she AUTOMATICALLY begins to what?

_____

_____

_____

_____

_____

# #1: I AM THE PRIZE

What powerful mindset dramatically improved my dating life? What did I quit believing?

_____
_____
_____
_____
_____

Seeing yourself as the prize in no way means you're what?

_____
_____
_____
_____
_____

When you see yourself as the prize, how are you supposed to see and treat women?

_____
_____
_____
_____
_____

When you're the prize, you are a valuable man who's spent more time and energy than the average person doing what?

_____

_____

_____

_____

_____

Why do your time, peace of mind, and happiness come first?

_____

_____

_____

_____

_____

When you're the prize, you communicate to women that...

_____

_____

_____

_____

_____

For the "I am the prize" mindset to work, you HAVE TO stop doing what?

_____

_____

_____

_____

_____

# #2: MY PURPOSE, GOALS, AND OPPORTUNITES COME FIRST

Men who sacrifice their purpose and opportunities in life to chase women will NEVER have what?

_____

_____

_____

_____

_____

The men who chase their purpose and take full advantage of opportunities will always have what?

_____

_____

_____

_____

_____

If you spend too much time and energy focusing on women instead of putting action behind bettering yourself, your life, and your career, what is likely to happen?

_____

_____

_____

_____

_____

The more effective mindset, one that'll make you happier, is...

_____

_____

_____

_____

_____

Realistically, when your life is on the right track and you're having a lot of success, you won't have to what? Why is this?

_____

_____

_____

_____

_____

The majority of successful men who have a great life spent most, if not all, of their time focused on what?

_____

_____

_____

_____

_____

Their wife, or whatever women they're with, usually came into their life when?

_____

_____

_____

_____

_____

Focusing on your purpose and opportunities above all else puts you in what position?

_____

_____

_____

_____

_____

The more you neglect your purpose, the more you…

_____

_____

_____

_____

_____

# #3: MY HAPPINESS COMES FIRST

Where do you draw the line in any kind of relationship?

_____

_____

_____

_____

_____

When you're not as happy or comfortable as you could be but you stay with that person or in that situation anyways, you're only doing what to yourself?

_____

_____

_____

_____

_____

When your happiness is more important to you than "comfort" and status, you'll what?

_____

_____

_____

_____

_____

When you put your own happiness first, how is it obvious to women?

_____

_____

_____

_____

_____

It doesn't matter how hot she is, how nice she is, or anything else about her, it's not your job to what?

_____

_____

_____

_____

_____

The men who are the most attractive to women are the ones who aren't what?

_____

_____

_____

_____

_____

# #4: IT'S NOT AS BIG OF A DEAL AS MOST PEOPLE MAKE IT

Most people aren't getting the results they want in life because they're what?

_____

_____

_____

_____

_____

The guys embarrassing themselves with women, that might include you, are doing what?

_____

_____

_____

_____

_____

It's extremely important to be consistent in the way you what?

_____

_____

_____

_____

_____

The men getting excellent results with women aren't doing what?

_____

_____

_____

_____

_____

When stressed, you are more attractive when you do what?

_____

_____

_____

_____

_____

# #5: I DON'T TAKE IT PERSONALLY WHEN SHE'S UPSET

It's OK if women get upset at you because at least while she's upset, she's what?

_____

_____

_____

_____

_____

Here's the simple truth, 99% of the women you'll meet, regardless of how much they like you, are going to do what?

_____

_____

_____

_____

_____

When she gets upset and starts shutting down or losing it, that's your golden opportunity to...

_____

_____

_____

_____

_____

What is the very best way to handle when women get upset?

_____

_____

_____

_____

_____

Why is getting upset when she's upset a really dumb thing to do?

_____

_____

_____

_____

_____

The better and more attractive way to handle her being upset, obviously, is to do what?

_____

_____

_____

_____

_____

In the long-term, it is 100X more attractive to be the guy who is...

_____

_____

_____

_____

_____

The people who react to everything in life are what?

_____

_____

_____

_____

_____

Those who don't take it personally and don't let it bother them...

_____

_____

_____

_____

_____

# #6 I DON'T TAKE IT PERSONALLY WHEN WOMEN DON'T LIKE ME

Why won't everyone like you when they first meet you? Why is this ok?

_____

_____

_____

_____

_____

If you struggle to accept that not all people are going to like you and worship you, then you are going to consistently struggle with what?

_____

_____

_____

_____

_____

Even if you're built like a Greek god and look like a male model from the magazines, a lot of women will still what?

_____

_____

_____

_____

_____

Being obsessed with what women think about you blocks your ability to what? What happens instead?

_____

_____

_____

_____

_____

_____

_____

_____

_____

The reason you have a problem with the idea of people not liking you is because...

_____

_____

_____

_____

_____

The more time and energy you put into getting people to like you and think you're a great guy, the more you what?

_____

_____

_____

_____

_____

The biggest secret I've ever learned about getting people to like you is...

_____

_____

_____

_____

_____

The guys who attract the most women are the ones who are...

_____

_____

_____

_____

_____

## What don't they do?

_____

_____

_____

_____

_____

# #7 I DON'T WASTE TIME ON PEOPLE WHO DON'T RESPECT ME OR ADD VALUE TO MY LIFE

A big part of getting your act together and attracting better women into your life is...

_____
_____
_____
_____
_____

What do these people do and why?

_____
_____
_____
_____
_____

Every second you spend on anyone who doesn't take you seriously costs who and why?

_____
_____
_____
_____
_____

When you shift your mindset to no longer wasting time on anyone who isn't worthy of it, the women who actually care about you will do what?

_____

_____

_____

_____

_____

At the same time, when you make that important shift, the women who aren't worth your time will do what?

_____

_____

_____

_____

_____

When you think and operate a certain way and you're clear about what you want, you will automatically...

_____

_____

_____

_____

_____

Whatever and whomever you want in your life, you have to become...

_____

_____

_____

_____

_____

# #8 I LIKE TO BE IN CONTROL

In order to get the results you actually want with women and for your life to go the way you want it to, you have to do what?

_____

_____

_____

_____

_____

Whatever and whomever you want in your life, you have to…

_____

_____

_____

_____

_____

The only people complaining are the ones who are what?

_____

_____

_____

_____

_____

Women feel more attraction and respect for the guy who is what?

_____

_____

_____

_____

_____

# #9 THE WORLD IS ABUNDANT

If you honestly believe that there are only so many single women to date and only so many opportunities to meet that perfect woman, then what is the problem?

_____
_____
_____
_____
_____

The truth is that...

_____
_____
_____
_____
_____

The abundance mindset is understanding there is...

_____
_____
_____
_____
_____

The only other roadblocks you face are...

_____
_____
_____
_____
_____

The abundance factor only activates in your life when you what?

_____
_____
_____
_____
_____

# #10 NO TIME FOR NEGATIVITY

The effect being positive has on women is profound and it makes them what?

_____

_____

_____

_____

_____

The more negativity you allow, the more you're doing what to your own mind?

_____

_____

_____

_____

_____

The more negativity you allow to come out of your mouth, the more you're doing what to yourself?

_____

_____

_____

_____

_____

Small, weak, and defeated minds focus on what?

_____

_____

_____

_____

_____

It's easier for weaker and smaller minds to...

_____

_____

_____

_____

_____

# CONCLUSION: MEN WHO WANT TO CONTINUOUSLY IMPROVE ATTRACT MORE WOMEN

How many books does the average American read per year?

_____

_____

_____

_____

_____

How many does the average CEO read?

_____

_____

_____

_____

_____

The person always striving to improve does WAY better than...

_____

_____

_____

_____

_____

The typical guy who's slaying it with women, that means doing good, and he isn't rich or unusually good-looking is in one way or another doing what?

_____

_____

_____

_____

_____

A man who has no interest in improving his mindset, behavior, and life only attracts what kind of women?

_____

_____

_____

_____

_____

What is their relationship with these women likely to look like?

_____

_____

_____

_____

_____

If you want more out of your dating life and out of life, what do you have to start doing?

_____

_____

_____

_____

_____

Something _____ will always happen in your life when you cram your brain full of positive information and only _____ things will happen when you cram your brain full of negative information. It's that simple.

If you want more women in your life and women who are more mature, caring, respectful, and less-problematic, you have to...

_____

_____

_____

_____

_____

Mindset trumps _____!

Improving your mindset will do what?

_____

_____

_____

_____

_____

The more you improve your mindset and everything about yourself, the more...

_____

_____

_____

_____

_____

# 2nd Edition

# HOW ATTRACTING WOMEN REALLY WORKS

*by Marc Summers*

Thank you for using this workbook and I hope I was able to expand your mind, help you out, and solve a lot of problems for you. Keep in mind that workbooksbooks like this are more helpful and effective when you actually fill them out completely and DO THE WORK to plant this information into your mind. I invest a lot of hours into putting each one of these workbooks together and if I missed anything or there's something you believe I can improve, do not hesitate to email me at **marc@majorleaguedating.com** and let me know. Once again, thank you very much for taking the time to use this workbook and if I didn't have your continued support, I wouldn't be able to continually push myself to create new content and find new ways to help you as much as possible. It's with great humility that I thank you from the bottom of my heart and wish you the very best of luck in accomplishing your goals. I am forever grateful for you. Please take a minute to check out my other products that'll help you out just as much as this one did.

# PLEASE REVIEW THIS BOOK:

Hey, it's Marc. Thank you very much for reading this book. If it helped you understand women, dating, and attraction better and believe it'll help you solve a lot of problems, **please go to amazon.com and leave me a 5 star review and positive feedback for this book**. It only takes 10 seconds and helps me more than you know. Thank you again.

*- Marc Summers*

## Customer Reviews

⭐⭐⭐⭐⭐ 71

4.9 out of 5 stars ▾

| | | |
|---|---|---|
| 5 star | ▮▮▮▮▮ | 92% |
| 4 star | ▮ | 7% |
| 3 star | | 1% |
| 2 star | | 0% |
| 1 star | | 0% |

Share your thoughts

Write a customer review

See all 71 customer reviews ›

Made in United States
Cleveland, OH
01 March 2025

14777749R10134